STRESS A
EMPLOYER LIA

Jill Earnshaw is a senior lecturer in employment law at the Manchester School of Management, University of Manchester Institute of Science and Technology (UMIST). As well as being a qualified barrister, she has an MSc in management sciences and wide experience of presenting legal issues in conferences and seminars to HR professionals and other non-specialists. For several years, she has also been a part-time chairman of employment tribunals. She co-edited and contributed to a book on vulnerable workers, and has written and broadcast widely on stress litigation, sexual harassment and changing employment patterns.

Cary L. Cooper is professor of organisational psychology at the Manchester School of Management, and Pro-Vice-Chancellor (External Activities) of the University of Manchester Institute of Science and Technology (UMIST). He is the author of over 80 books and over 300 articles for academic journals. A frequent contributor to national newspapers, TV and radio, he is editor-in-chief of the *Journal of Organizational Behavior* and co-editor of the medical journal, *Stress Medicine*. He is also a fellow of the British Psychological Society and of the Royal Society of Arts. His book *HR Know-How in Mergers and Acquisitions* (with Dr Sue Cartwright) was published by the CIPD in 2000.

Other titles in the series:

The Chartered Institute of Personnel and Development is the leading publisher of books and reports for personnel and training professionals, students, and for all those concerned with the effective management and development of people at work. For details of all our titles, please contact the Publishing Department:

tel. 020-8263 3387
fax 020-8263 3850
e-mail publish@cipd.co.uk
The catalogue of all CIPD titles can be viewed on the CIPD website:
www.cipd.co.uk/publications

STRESS AND EMPLOYER LIABILITY

Second edition

Jill Earnshaw
and
Cary L. Cooper

Chartered Institute of Personnel and Development

First edition published 1996
Reprinted 1997
Second edition published 2001

Design by Paperweight
Typeset by The Comp-Room, Aylesbury
Printed in Great Britain by
The Cromwell Press, Trowbridge

British Library Cataloguing in Publication Data
A catalogue record for this book is available from the
British Library

ISBN 0-85292-878-5

The views expressed in this book are the authors' own, and
may not necessarily reflect those of the CIPD.

Chartered Institute of Personnel and Development,
CIPD House, Camp Road, London SW19 4UX
Tel: 020 8971 9000   Fax: 020 8263 3333
E-mail: cipd@cipd.co.uk
Website: www.cipd.co.uk
Incorporated by Royal Charter. Registered charity no. 1079797

CONTENTS

LIST OF ABBREVIATIONS

ACAS	Advisory, Conciliation and Arbitration Service
ACTR	Australian Capital Territory Reports
All ER	All England Law Reports
CBI	Confederation of British Industry
DDA	Disability Discrimination Act 1995
DSM-IV	The American Diagnostic and Statistical Manual of Mental Disorders
DSS	Department of Social Security
EAP	Employment Assistance Programme
EAT	Employment Appeal Tribunal
EOC	Equal Opportunities Commission
EU	European Union
HASAWA	Health and Safety at Work Act 1974
HSE	Health and Safety Executive
ICD-10	The International Classification of Diseases and Related Health Problems
ICR	Industrial Cases Reports
IRLR	Industrial Relations Law Reports
LR	Law Reports
MHSW	Management of Health and Safety at Work Regulations 1992
NHS	National Health Service
NLJ	New Law Journal
PIQR	Personal Injuries and Quantum Reports
PTSD	Post-traumatic stress disorder
RRA	Race Relations Act 1976
RSI	Repetitive strain injury
SDA	Sex Discrimination Act 1975
WLR	Weekly Law Reports
YTS	Youth Training Scheme

ACKNOWLEDGEMENTS

We should like to express our thanks to the following:

- FOCUS Ltd for sponsoring our research into stress litigation
- Vicky Atkinson for allowing us to use the data obtained for the purpose of her MSc dissertation
- Stuart Esworthy for giving us access to his dissertation on 'Post-traumatic stress disorder: prevention and cure within building societies in Great Britain'
- Brian Doyle for his help on the disability discrimination section (although any remaining errors are of course our responsibility)
- Janet Denny for typing the manuscript and for her patience in carrying out numerous revisions and amendments
- those solicitors who spared the time from their busy practices to talk to us about their cases, especially:

Michael Connor	Robin Thompson and Partners, Stoke-on-Trent
David Franey	Russell, Jones and Walker, Manchester
Diane Hawkins	Whittles, Manchester
Karen Mitchell	Brian Thompson and Partners, Hull
Richard Morgan	Hulme & Co, Worcester
Richard Scorer	Pannone and Partners, Manchester
John Usher	Brian Thompson and Partners, Leeds
Fraser Whitehead	Russell, Jones and Walker, London

- last, but not least, all those individuals who allowed us to use their stories and pester them for relevant details that we thought we needed.

The law is stated as at the end of June 2000.

1 INTRODUCTION

The context of workplace stress

Over the past decades, many factors have conspired to make working life far more stressful than before. During the 1980s the 'enterprise culture' helped to transform the UK economy. Yet we soon discovered substantial personal costs in terms of major redundancies, heavier workloads, longer working hours, greater job insecurity, and increased pressures of work impinging on the family and on personal life. An Institute of Management survey found that a large number of managers in the UK were distressed by their long working hours (77 per cent) and by the effect of their work on their family life (77 per cent), and were significantly worried about how this was affecting their relationship with their partners (74 per cent). In other words, 'stress' had found a firm place in our modern business vocabulary alongside 'junk bonds', 'e-mail', and 'golden parachutes'.

In a sense, the 1980s was a decade of 'self-induced stress', a time when individuals pushed themselves towards the edge to achieve personal success and material gain. However, the end of the 1980s and the beginning of the 1990s were characterised instead by 'imposed stress', as companies attempted to survive the recession by cutting their labour costs through downsizing (or, as Americans now colloquially call it, 'right-sizing'), dumping more work on fewer shoulders and encouraging a culture of organisational commitment through long working hours. At the same time, the UK economy was shifting rapidly towards an almost wholly privatised culture in the public sector and the outsourcing of many activities within private-sector companies. This has led to a new phase of organisational life that may be termed the 'contract culture', one likely to have more profound effects on working people than either the enterprise culture or the downsizing activities of the recession.

Short-term contracts and part-time working are becoming the order of the day. In the last quarter of 1994, for example, over 74,000 full-time jobs were lost, whereas 173,000 part-time jobs were created. One in eight UK workers is now self-employed, and many more men are working part-time (the numbers doubled over the period 1984 to 1994). This new 'flexible workforce' is anything but family-friendly, and the psychological contract between employer and employee – which traditionally offered 'reasonably permanent employment for work well done' – is truly being undermined, as more and more employees no longer regard their employment as secure; many more are engaged in part-time working. Indeed, in the International Survey Research (ISR) report on 400 companies in 17 countries employing over 8 million workers throughout Europe, the employment security of workers significantly declined between 1985 and 1995: UK, from 70 per cent in 1985 to 48 per cent in 1995; Germany, from 83 to 55 per cent; France, from 64 to 50 per cent; the Netherlands, from 73 to 61 per cent; Belgium, from 60 to 54 per cent; and Italy from 62 to 57 per cent. In fact, in the 2000 ISR survey, it was found that 'attitudes towards employment security are the only area in which there has been a significant decline across Europe'.[1]

It could be argued that there is nothing inherently wrong with this trend, but three recent Quality of Working Life Surveys by the Institute of Management and UMIST (which annually surveys a cohort of 5,000 British managers) found some disturbing results.[2] In 1997, 1998 and 1999, over 60 per cent of this national sample had undergone a major restructuring over the last 12 months involving major downsizing and outsourcing. The consequences of this change, even among an occupational group (ie middle and senior managers) supposedly in control of events, were that nearly two out of three experienced increased job insecurity, lowered morale, and the erosion of motivation and loyalty.

Most of these changes involved downsizing, cost reduction, de-layering and outsourcing. Yet the perception was that, although these changes invariably led to an increase in profitability and productivity, decision-making was slower and, more importantly, the organisation was deemed to have lost the right mix of human resource skills and experience in the process.

In addition, the impact on working patterns was penal, both from a business point of view and in terms of managers' outside lives. This was due not only to more work being loaded on the metaphorical 'backs of fewer managers', but also to 'presenteeism', the need for managers to demonstrate commitment by working longer and unsocial hours – behaviour that they feel (possibly wrongly) will protect them from the next wave of redundancies. It was found, in the 1999 survey, that over three out of four managers in the UK regularly worked more than their contracted hours each week, with over 54 per cent reporting working often or always every evening and over 34 per cent always or often working over the weekends. What is even more worrying is that by 1999 60 per cent felt these excessive hours *adversely* affected their morale, 68 per cent their productivity, 71 per cent their health, a troubling 79 per cent their relationship with their partner/spouse and 86 per cent their relationship with their children.

Stress in the workplace, however, is primarily caused by the fundamentals of change, lack of control and high workload. The build-up and aftermath of the recession, the European Union (EU), increasing cross-national mergers, growing international competition, joint ventures between organisations across boundaries, and the movement towards short-term contracts and part-time working will all inevitably lead to a variety of corporate "re-'s": reorganisation, relocation of personnel, redesign of jobs, and reallocation of roles and responsibilities. Change has been the password of the mid- to late 1990s, with its accompanying job insecurities, corporate culture clashes, and significantly different styles of managerial leadership: in other words, massive organisational change and the inevitable stress that it involves. In addition, this change will bring with it a larger-scale workload as companies try to create 'lean, fighting machines' to compete in the European and international arenas. This will mean fewer people to do more work, which will put enormous pressure on existing employees.

Finally, as we move away from the UK and enter larger economic systems, individual organisations will have less control over their business life. Rules and regulations have increasingly been imposed in terms of labour laws, and health and safety at work, and may soon begin to cover methods of production, distribution and remuneration. These may all be laudable in their own right, but they are nevertheless workplace constraints that will inhibit individual control and autonomy. Without wishing to be too gloomy, we have in the first decade of the new millennium, therefore, all the ingredients of corporate stress: an ever-increasing workload with a decreasing workforce in a climate of rapid change, with control over the means of production increasingly taken over by pan-European bureaucracies (whether the EU or some larger entity in the longer term).

It appears that stress is not just a bygone remnant of the entrepreneurial 1980s but is here to stay, and the purpose of this book is to explore this phenomenon in the context of employer liability for stress at work. Although a great deal has been written in recent years about the sources of stress, less attention has been focused on what the implications of this are in terms of employee litigation and stress management and prevention.

The growing legal threat

From the beginning of the 1990s, research into workplace stress (which has increasingly linked it to specific features of the working environment) highlighted the possibility of legal claims. There seemed no logical reason why stress-induced illness should be treated differently from any other work-related disease or injury, and why, therefore, it should not lead to personal injury claims against employers who failed to take reasonable steps to guard against it.

The experience in the USA of the operation of the Workers' Compensation Scheme also increased awareness of the possibility of such litigation. Unlike personal injury actions in the UK, it is a no-fault insurance scheme designed to compensate for work-related accidents and injuries, but statistics show that it has been deluged with floods of claims relating to mental as opposed to physical injury.[3] During the 1980s alone, there was a tripling in the number of 'cumulative trauma' claims arising out of breakdowns in health caused by continual stress at work over prolonged periods of time.[4]

Employers and their insurers were repeatedly warned by both academic researchers and articles in the press that it was only a matter of time before we saw a parallel development in the UK.[5] Headlines such as 'Insurers fear stress claims will increase',

'Overworked? Under Pressure? Insurers fear you could soon be suing for millions', and 'Pressure mounts on stress' appeared with monotonous regularity and it was reported that the Health and Safety Executive was to issue guidelines on workplace stress, establishing it firmly as a health and safety matter. Then in 1991, Chris Johnstone, a junior medical officer, sued Bloomsbury Health Authority in respect of his mental break-down, allegedly caused by long working hours. Although his claim for compensation was settled out of court, the associated media coverage alerted many organisations to the very real threat they faced. In 1995 that threat was realised by the successful personal injury action brought by a social worker, John Walker, against Northumberland County Council (see pages 37–38).

Since then, a number of substantial out-of-court settlements have been reported in the press. In 1996 a teacher received £82,000 from Coventry City Council following an assault on her by a pupil[6] and in 1998 there were pay-outs of £100,000 to a policeman who was demoted following a series of poor staff appraisals[7] and to a deputy headteacher who suffered two nervous breakdowns as a result of bullying.[8] In the same year, the widow of a male nurse who committed suicide after being forced to take on managerial tasks with which he could not cope, agreed to a settlement of £25,000[9] and more recently Birmingham County Court awarded £67,400 to a City Council worker when her employers admitted liability for her forced medical retirement caused by their failure to provide her with managerial support on her promotion.[10]

The structure of the book

Chapters 2 and 3 lay the foundation for the legal discussions in later chapters by attempting both a definition of stress and an indication of how stress can affect health detrimentally. They also describe the sources of workplace stress as demonstrated by research over the last decade, and its cost to organisations.

Chapter 4 discusses in detail the way in which personal injury claims based on workplace stress fit into the framework of the law on negligence. It emphasises that employers' duties to guard against psychiatric harm arise once such harm is foreseeable, but that what is expected from employers is only a reasonable response. In the belief that future legal claims may arise out of traumatic workplace experiences (including bullying), in addition to more chronic stressors such as over-work and long working hours, some space is devoted to post-traumatic stress disorder (PTSD) and the complex state of the law in relation to 'nervous shock'. Relevant legal issues such as 'foreseeability' and 'causation' (ie that the stress-induced injury was caused by the working environment) are illustrated wherever possible by reference to the *Walker* case or other related case law.

Statutory duties and potential criminal liability under long-standing health and safety legislation are scrutinised in Chapter 5. It begins by outlining relevant duties under the Health and Safety at Work Act (HASAWA) 1974 and the explicit require-ment to carry out risk assessments introduced by the Manage-ment of Health and Safety at Work (MHSW) Regulations 1992. If mental and physical well-being are now to be equated, employers who fail in their duty to protect employees against psychiatric harm may, in theory at least, face prosecution. This chapter also points out that claims may arise under employ-ment protection legislation and statutes outlawing discrimina-tion on grounds of race and sex. Although the Employment Rights Act (ERA) 1996 allows employers to dismiss those who, because of a stress-related illness, are incapable of doing their job, dismissals that are mismanaged are likely to result in claims of unfair dismissal. Constructive dismissal claims may likewise arise where employees become so stressed by aspects of their work or working environment that they feel obliged to resign.

Discrimination legislation is included in this chapter too, because it is very often the case that those who are subjected to discrimination on grounds of sex or race, especially where that takes the form of harassment, suffer psychological conse-quences. Employment tribunals are increasingly recognising this by awarding substantial sums of compensation for injury to feelings and it has now been confirmed that they also have the power to award damages for personal injury in such cases. Chapter 5 concludes by noting that the new disability discrimi-nation legislation may have implications in this area, because mental disability is specifically included in the Act.

Chapter 6 details the results of brief survey questionnaires and follow-up interviews designed to explore the sort of legal claims that have found their way to the doors of personal injury solicitors. It highlights the worrying finding, borne out by the case studies also included in the chapter, that many claims are based, in effect, on allegations of bullying, variously described as persecution, victimisation and pressure management. It also reveals that claims are arising in a variety of occupations and industrial sectors.

Whereas earlier chapters may have caused employers some alarm, Chapter 7 sets out to indicate what steps can be taken to minimise liability by preventing stressful situations from arising or by dealing with them effectively if they do arise. It points out that any preventive measures must be preceded by a proper assessment of risks to mental well-being, which will vary substantially from one organisation to another. Remedial techniques such as stress-management programmes and employee counselling are also canvassed, with illustrations of successful attempts to deal with stress in a sample of organisations.

Chapter 8 rounds off the book by giving some thought to future developments, and covers some of the more practical considerations, such as limitation periods and levels of damages.

In essence, then, this book aims to raise awareness of the question of liability for workplace stress and to explore the relevant legal issues. An attempt is made throughout to avoid unnecessary legal jargon, so that 'lay' experts in their own fields (such as human resource managers and occupational health professionals) will find it readily accessible. However, we hope it will equally be of interest to lawyers who may be familiar with personal injury actions in general but have a limited knowledge of psychiatric harm and workplace stress. In so far as it beneficially affects the day-to-day lives of working people, we shall claim it to have been a success.

References

1 International Survey Research. *Tracking Trends: Employee satisfaction in Europe*. London, International Survey Research, 2000.
2 Worrall L. and Cooper C. L. *Quality of Working Life Survey*. London, Institute of Management, 1997–9.

3 NIOSH. *Proposed National Strategies for the Prevention of Leading Work-Related Disease and Injuries*. Cincinnati, National Institute of Occupational Safety and Health, 1986.

4 Karasek R. and Theorell T. *Healthy Work: Stress, productivity and the reconstruction of working life*. New York, Basic Books, 1990.

5 Earnshaw J. M. and Cooper C. L. 'Workmen's compensation in stress-related claims: some thoughts for employers in the UK'. *Work and Stress*. Vol. 5(3). pp253–7. 1991.

6 *New Law Practitioner*. 9 August. pp1, 211. 1996.

7 Daily Telegraph. 'Ex-detective wins claim for years of stress'. 9 May. p9. 1998.

8 Lightfoot L. 'I got to the point where I couldn't teach'. *Daily Telegraph*. 17 July. p3. 1998.

9 *Health Law*. 'Stress at Work'. Vol. 3(3). March. pp5–6. 1998

10 Johnstone H. 'Woman is awarded £67,000 for stress'. *The Times*. 6 July. p7. 1999.

2   OCCUPATIONAL STRESS AND ITS EFFECT ON HEALTH

Defining stress

'Stress' is derived from Latin *stringere*, meaning 'to draw tight', and was used in the seventeenth century to describe hardships or affliction. During the late eighteenth century, stress denoted 'force, pressure, strain or strong effort', referring primarily to an individual, or to the individual's organs or mental powers.[1]

Early definitions of strain and load in physics and engineering eventually came to influence one concept of how stress affects individuals. Under this concept, external forces (load) are seen as exerting pressure upon an individual, producing strain. Proponents of this view argue that we can measure the stress to which an individual is subjected in the same way as we can measure physical strain on a machine or bridge, or any physical object.

Whereas this first concept looked at stress as an outside stimulus, a second concept defines it as a person's response to a disturbance. As early as 1910, Sir William Osler explored the idea of stress and strain causing 'disease' when he saw a relationship between angina pectoris and a hectic pace of life. The idea that environmental forces could actually cause disease, rather than just short-term ill effects, and that people have a natural tendency to resist such forces, was seen in the work of Walter B. Cannon in the 1930s. Cannon studied the effects of stress upon animals and people, and in particular the 'fight or flight' reaction. Through this reaction, people, as well as animals, choose whether to stay and fight or to try to escape when confronting extreme danger. Cannon observed that when his subjects experienced situations of cold, lack of oxygen, and excitement he could detect such physiological changes as emergency adrenaline secretions. Cannon described these individuals as being 'under stress'.

One of the first scientific attempts to explain the process of stress-related illness was made in 1946 by Hans Selye, who described three stages that an individual encounters in stressful situations:

1 alarm reaction, in which an initial phase of lowered resistance is followed by countershock, during which the individual's defence mechanisms become active

2 resistance, the stage of maximum adaptation and, hopefully, successful return to equilibrium for the individual; if, however, the stress agent continues or the defence mechanism does not work, he or she will move on to the third stage, described below

3 exhaustion, when adaptive mechanisms collapse.

Newer and more comprehensive theories of stress emphasise the interaction between a person and his or her environment.

Richard S. Lazarus of the University of California has suggested that an individual's stress reaction 'depends on how the person interprets or appraises (consciously or unconsciously) the significance of a harmful, threatening or challenging event'. Lazarus disagrees with those who see stress simply as environmental pressure. Instead:

> the intensity of the stress experience is determined significantly by how well a person feels he/she can cope with an identified threat. If a person is unsure of his/her coping abilities, they are likely to feel helpless and overwhelmed.[2]

Similarly, Tom Cox of Nottingham University has suggested that stress can best be understood as 'part of a complex and dynamic system of transaction between the person and his environment'.[3]

By looking at stress as the result of a misfit between an individual and his or her particular environment, we can begin to understand why one person seems to flourish in a certain setting while another suffers. Cary Cooper of the University of Manchester Institute of Science and Technology (UMIST) and Tom Cummings of the University of Southern California have designed a way of understanding the stress process, which can be explained thus:

☐ Individuals, for the most part, try to keep their thoughts, emotions and relationships with the world in a 'steady state'.

☐ Each factor of a person's emotional and physical state has a 'range of stability' in which that person feels comfortable. On the other hand, when forces disrupt one of these factors beyond the range of stability, the individual must act to restore a feeling of comfort.

☐ An individual's behaviour aimed at maintaining a steady state makes up his or her 'adjustment process' or coping strategies.

'Stress' is any force that puts a psychological or physical factor beyond its range of stability, producing strain within the individual. Knowledge that stress is likely to occur constitutes a threat to the individual. A threat can cause strain because of what it signifies to the person.[4] As can be seen, the idea of stress and its effects upon people has evolved from different research perspectives. Figure 1 summarises these different approaches into an overview of the concept of stress.

Figure 1 **THE COOPER-CUMMINGS FRAMEWORK**

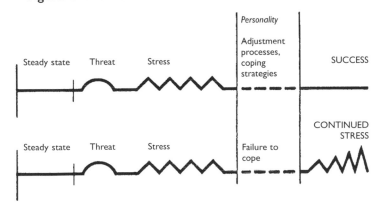

As stress begins to take its toll on the body and the mind a variety of symptoms can result. Researchers have identified a range of behavioural and physical symptoms of stress that commonly occurs before the onset of more serious stress-related illnesses.[5] Table 1 indicates the behavioural and physical symptoms usually associated with some stressor in life.

Table 1 **BEHAVIOURAL AND PHYSICAL SYMPTOMS OF STRESS**

Behavioural symptoms of stress
Constant irritability with people
Difficulty in making decisions
Loss of sense of humour
Suppressed anger
Difficulty concentrating
Inability to finish one task before rushing into another
Feeling one is the target of others' animosity
Feeling unable to cope
Wanting to cry at the smallest problem
Lack of interest in doing things after return home from work
Waking up in the morning and feeling tired after an early night
Constant tiredness.

Physical symptoms of stress
Lack of appetite
Craving for food when under pressure
Frequent indigestion or heartburn
Constipation or diarrhoea
Insomnia
Tendency to sweat for no good reason
Nervous twitches, nail-biting, etc
Headaches
Cramps and muscle spasms
Nausea
Breathlessness without exertion
Fainting spells
Impotence or frigidity
Eczema.

In addition, many physicians have identified a range of illnesses in which stress either plays a role or is one of the major risk factors (see Table 2).[6]

Table 2 LIST OF AILMENTS RECOGNISED TO HAVE POSSIBLE STRESS BACKGROUND

Hypertension: high blood pressure	Menstrual difficulties
Coronary thrombosis: heart attack	Nervous dyspepsia:
Migraine	flatulence and
Hay fever and allergies	indigestion
Asthma	Hyperthyroidism:
Pruritis: intense itching	overactive thyroid gland
Peptic ulcers	Diabetes mellitus
Constipation	Skin disorders
Colitis	Tuberculosis
Rheumatoid arthritis	Depression

All these symptoms and manifestations of ill-health stem from our primitive 'fight or flight' response, which produces surges of biochemical reactions that can lead to physiological problems. In fact, modern man has retained his primitive hormonal and chemical defence mechanisms intact through the centuries.[7, 8] But, for the most part, our lifestyle today does not allow physical reaction to the stress agents we face. Attacking the boss, slugging an insolent clerk, or smashing an empty automatic cash dispenser are not solutions allowed by today's society. Today, even the non-aggressive 'flight' reaction would hardly be judged appropriate in most situations. The executive who flees from a tense meeting, or the assembly worker who dashes out in the middle of a shift, will probably suffer the consequences of their actions. Our long-evolved defence mechanisms prepare us for dramatic and rapid action, but find little outlet.

It is this frustration of our natural response to stress that may actually harm us. Although scientists do not fully understand the process, it is believed that our thought patterns regarding ourselves and the situations we are in trigger events within two branches of our central nervous system: the 'sympathetic' and the 'parasympathetic'. As Albrecht describes it, in a situation of challenge, tension or pressure the sympathetic nervous system 'comes into play and activates a virtual orchestra of hormone secretions'.[9] It is through this activation that the hypothalamus, recognising a danger, triggers the pituitary gland. The pituitary releases hormones, causing the adrenal glands to intensify the output of adrenaline into the bloodstream. This adrenaline, along with corticosteroid hormones released through the same process, enhances one's level of arousal. All these stress chemicals stimulate the cognitive, neurological, cardiovascular and muscular systems.

Whereas these changes are the result of the role of the sympathetic branch, the parasympathetic branch can induce a state of relaxation and tranquillity. As Albrecht notes, 'people who have spent much of their time in an over-anxious or tense state have difficulty in bringing into action the parasympathetic branch' and its helpful abilities.

All of the body's 'rev-up' activity is designed to improve performance. But, researchers believe, if the stress that launches this activity continues unabated, the human body begins to weaken as it is bombarded by stimulation and stress-related chemicals. Melhuish[10] has described many of the long-term effects of pressure in Table 3.

Heart disease and hypertension

Stress plays a part in diseases related to lifestyle, where the degree to which a person eats, smokes, drinks alcohol and exercises is a significant factor. The first two illnesses in the list of ailments in Table 2, high blood pressure and heart attacks, are accepted now as having a proven link to stress. Hypertension, or raised blood pressure, has in most cases no direct organic basis – it simply sets in. A majority of cases are diagnosed as 'essential hypertension', meaning that they do not arise from any medically correctable function.

Although other factors such as diet, obesity and smoking surely play a significant role, many researchers now believe stress is a central cause of hypertension. The connection, as Melhuish indicates, is as follows: hypertension is believed to result partially from changes in the resistance of the blood vessels. The tension of the arterial vessels, which carry blood to the tissues, is partly controlled by the sympathetic nervous system and its release of chemicals through the vessels. Continual activation of the sympathetic nervous system's chemical response is believed to result in reduced elasticity of the arteries and raised blood pressure. This resulting hypertension can lead to heart disease because of the increased workload on the heart as it pushes blood out against a high arterial pressure. Chronic stress, and its consequent release of fats into the bloodstream

Table 3 EFFECTS OF STRESS ON BODILY FUNCTIONS

	Normal (relaxed)	Under pressure	Acute pressure	Chronic pressure (stress)
Brain	Blood supply normal	Blood supply up	Thinks more clearly	Headaches and migraines, tremors and nervous tics
Mood	Happy	Serious	Increased concentration	Anxiety, loss of sense of humour
Saliva	Normal	Reduced	Reduced	Dry mouth, lump in throat
Muscles	Blood supply normal	Blood supply up	Improved performance	Muscular tension and pain
Heart	Normal rate and blood pressure	Increased rate and blood pressure	Improved performance	Hypertension and chest pain
Lungs	Normal respiration	Increased respiration rate	Improved performance	Coughs and asthma
Stomach	Normal blood supply and acid secretion	Reduced blood supply and increased acid secretion	Reduced blood supply reduces digestion	Ulcers due to heartburn and indigestion
Bowels	Normal blood supply and bowel activity	Reduced blood supply and increased bowel activity	Reduced blood supply reduces digestion	Abdominal pain and diarrhoea
Bladder	Normal	Frequent urination	Frequent urination due to increased nervous stimulation	Frequent urination, prostatic symptoms
Sexual organs	(Male) Normal (Female) Normal periods, etc	(Male) Impotence (decreased blood supply) (Female) Irregular periods	Decreased blood supply	(Male) Impotence (Female) Menstrual disorders
Skin	Healthy	Decreased blood supply, dry skin	Decreased blood supply	Dryness and rashes
Biochemistry	Normal: oxygen consumed, glucose and fats liberated	Oxygen consumption up, glucose and fat consumption up	More energy immediately available	Rapid tiredness

Source: A. Melhuish, *Executive Health*, London, Business Books, 1978.

during the 'fight or flight' response, is also believed to increase the risk of coronary heart disease by adding fatty deposits to the lining of the coronary arteries, which provide oxygen to the heart muscle.

Cancer and the immune system

Some researchers are exploring the connection between stress and cancer, believing stress may cause a suppression of the immune system.[11] Fox suggests there are two primary mechanisms causing cancer: first, 'carcinogenesis, the production of cancer by an agent or mechanism overcoming existing resistance of the body'; and second, 'lowered resistance to cancer, which permits a potential carcinogen normally insufficient to produce cancer, to do so'.[12] In addition, recent research has identified behavioural and stress-related components in the onset of cancer.[13]

Stomach and intestinal problems

Certain individuals appear to respond to stress with an increase in the production of stomach acids, often contributing to ulcers of the stomach or duodenum (the first part of the small intestine). Other conditions believed to be brought on or aggravated by chronic stress include ulcerative colitis (bleeding ulcerations in the large intestine) and irritable bowel syndrome (painful spasms in the large intestine).[14]

Headaches and backache

Many headaches appear to be caused by tension in the muscles in the face and scalp. This type of headache, sometimes known as 'tension headache', is one of the commonest symptoms of stress. Certain headaches called migraines seem to result from spasms of blood vessels supplying the brain and appear to be connected to a variety of factors, possibly including stress. Similarly, backache is often attributed to stress-induced muscle spasms or to poor physical condition or inflexibility during work.

Skin problems

Skin diseases are a highly visible consequence of the aggravating effects of stress. Eczema, hives and acne are all skin conditions believed to be associated with stress. For example, one study demonstrated that 'in eczema-prone individuals, emotional arousal leads to specific changes in the skin cells'.[15]

In conclusion, as Cooper and Quick[16] suggest, stress is a risk factor to health when it occurs frequently or is too intense, prolonged or mismanaged. Stressful working environments and situations can pose a threat to both health and life.

> Stress, although not the only or primary cause, is implicated in over half of all human morbidity and mortality. In the USA and developed countries, the ten leading causes of death account for 79-80% of all deaths. Stress is directly implicated in four cases (heart disease, strokes, injuries, and suicide and homicide) and indirectly in a further three (cancer, chronic liver disease, and emphysema and chronic bronchitis). Common presenting symptoms are anxiety and depression.

The mental and physical health risks faced by each individual coping poorly with prolonged stress cannot be predicted exactly; it is clear, however, that the potential costs to the individual can be enormous. Before looking at how each person can analyse his or her own stress level, and act to reduce it, we shall take a closer look at the costs of stress to individuals.

References

1 Hinkle L. E. 'The concept of stress in biological social sciences'. *Stress Medicine and Man*. I. pp31–48. 1973.

2 Lazarus R. S. *Patterns of Adjustment*. New York, McGraw-Hill, 1976.

3 Cox T. *Stress*. London, Macmillan, 1978.

4 Cummings T. and Cooper C. L. 'A cybernetic framework for the study of occupational stress'. *Human Relations*. Vol. 32. pp395–419. 1979.

5 Cartwright S. and Cooper C. L. *Managing Workplace Stress*. London, Sage Publications, 1997.

6 Cooper C. L. *Handbook of Stress, Medicine and Health*. Boca Raton, Florida, CRC Press, 1996.

7 Melhuish A. *Executive Health*. London, Business Books, 1978.

8 Albrecht K. *Stress and the Manager: Making it work for you*. New Jersey, Prentice-Hall, 1979.

9 See note 8.

10 See note 7.

11 Cooper C. L. *Stress and Breast Cancer*. Chichester, John Wiley & Sons, 1988.

12 Fox B. H. 'Premorbid psychological factors'. *Journal of Behavioural Medicine*. Vol. I, (I). 1978.

13 Cooper C. L. and Watson M. *Cancer and Stress: Psychological, biological and coping studies*. Chichester, John Wiley & Sons, 1991.

14 Quick J. C. and Quick J. D. *Organizational Stress and Preventive Management*. New York, McGraw-Hill, 1984.

15 See note 14.

16 Cooper C. L. and Quick J. C. *Stress and Strain*. Oxford, Health Press, 1999.

3 WORKPLACE SOURCES OF STRESS

Introduction: the costs of stress

With a growing body of research evidence, there can be little dispute that stress has a dysfunctional impact on both individual and organisational outcomes.[1, 2] Links have been demonstrated between stress and the incidence of coronary heart disease, alcoholism, mental breakdown, poor health behaviours, job dissatisfaction, accidents, family problems and certain forms of cancer.[3, 4] For UK companies in the 1980s, stress in the workplace was 10 times more costly than industrial relations disputes. By the end of the 1990s, the costs had escalated even further. The Confederation of Business Industry[5] calculated the total costs to British business of sickness absence at £11 billion in the year 2000 alone, or a cost per employee of £438. Although minor illness was the single biggest cause, workplace stress was second, but the other main contributors were also stress-related sources such as personal problems, poor workplace morale, impact of long hours, lack of commitment, and drink and drug problems. If you aggregate all of these together with the workplace stress category, this umbrella construct of work-life stress is the biggest cause of sickness absence. The cost is likely to be in the order for UK plc of £5-6 billion per annum. In addition, the Health and Safety Executive (HSE) estimates that about 40 million working days per year are lost to all public- and private-sector organisations. According to the HSE, one in five employees admits to taking time off work because of work-related stress, and one in 13 consult their GP on stress-related problems. A 1997 survey by a long-term disability insurer according to the (then) Institute of Personnel and

Development found claims for compensation arising from mental problems had increased by 90 per cent in a five-year period. And finally, a large-scale survey in 1996 of 15,800 European workers, carried out by the European Foundation for the Improvement of Living and Working Conditions, showed that 28 per cent of European workers consider their health had been adversely affected by stress in the workplace. They also found two years later that 'high stress' working conditions had increased even further, with a noted increase particularly among women workers.

Certain countries (eg the USA) are showing declines in such stress-related illnesses as heart disease and alcoholism. In contrast, the World Health Organisation has published figures indicating that the UK is near the top of the world league table in terms of fatality due to heart disease. The British Heart Foundation has estimated that, each year, heart disease costs the average UK company of 10,000 employees: 73,000 lost working days; the death of 42 of its employees (between 35 and 64 years old); and lost productive value to its products or services of over £2.5 million.

The current cost of stress to the nation is also extremely high. For example, the British Heart Foundation Coronary Prevention Group has calculated that 180,000 people die in the UK each year from coronary heart disease, ie 500 people a day. In addition, MIND (the mental health charity) estimates that between 30 and 40 per cent of all sickness absence from work is attributable to mental and emotional disturbance. The country has also suffered from increased rates of suicide amongst the young, increasing by 30 per cent from the late 1970s to the early 1990s, particularly in the younger age groups of employees. Instability and life stress must be a major factor in annual divorce rates rising from 27,000 in 1961 to 171,000 by the late 1990s, and this upward trend continues. Currently in the UK there are roughly four divorces for every 10 marriages. Finally, Alcohol Concern estimates that one in four men in the UK drinks more than the medically recommended number of units per week, and that 25 per cent of accidents at work involve workers under the influence of alcohol. Society in general as well as UK plc is clearly suffering from stress.

Who pays the costs?

Why is it that many countries (eg the USA, Finland) seem to be showing lower levels of such stress-related illnesses as heart disease and alcoholism, while the UK's are still rising? Is it the case, for example, that US employers are becoming more altruistic and caring for their employees, and less concerned about 'the bottom line'? Unfortunately, the answer is likely to be no. Two trends in the USA are forcing firms there to take action. First, US industry is facing an enormous and ever-spiralling bill for employee health care costs. Individual insurance costs have risen by 50 per cent over the past two decades, but the employers' contribution has risen by more than 140 per cent. It has also been estimated that more than $700 million a year is spent by US employers to replace the 200,000 men aged from 45 to 65 who die from, or who are incapacitated by, coronary artery disease alone. Top management at Xerox estimated in the 1980s and early 1990s that losing just one executive to a stress-related illness costs the organisation $600,000. In the UK, however, employers can create intolerable levels of stress among their employees and leave it to the taxpayer to pick up the bill through the National Health Service (NHS). There is no direct accountability of, or incentive for, firms to maintain the health of their employees. Of course, the indirect costs are enormous, but rarely do firms actually attempt to estimate them; they treat absenteeism, labour turnover and even low productivity as an intrinsic part of running a business.[6]

Second, there is another source of growing costs. More and more employees, in US companies at least, are litigating against their employers, through the worker compensation regulations and laws, in respect of job-related stress, or what is being termed 'cumulative trauma'. In the UK we are beginning to see a similar move towards litigation by workers about their conditions of work. Several unions are supporting cases by individual workers, and the trend is certainly in the direction of mental disability claims and damages being awarded on the basis of workplace stress. This parallel trend will be the main focus of our book.

Sources of stress at work

During the 1980s much of the research in the field of workplace stress suggested that there are six major sources of pressure at work.[7] Although we can find each of these in an individual's stress profile or, indeed, in an organisation's profile, the factors vary in the degree to which they are found to be causally linked to stress in a particular job or organisation (see Figure 2).

Figure 2 DYNAMICS OF WORK STRESS

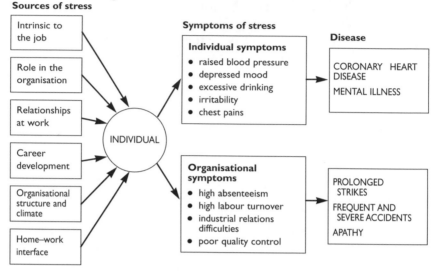

Factors intrinsic to the job

As a starting point to understanding work stress, researchers have studied those factors that may be intrinsic to the job itself, such as: poor working conditions; shift work; long hours; travel; risk and danger; new technology; and work overload – or indeed underload.

Working conditions

Our physical surroundings – noise, lighting, smells and all the stimuli that bombard our senses – can affect our moods and overall mental state, whether or not we consciously find them objectionable.[8] Each occupation has its own potential environmental sources of stress. For example, in jobs where individuals are dealing with close-detail work, poor lighting can create eye strain. Conversely, extremely bright lighting or glare can present problems for money-market dealers.

The design or physical setting of the workplace is another

potential source of stress. If an office is poorly designed, with personnel spread throughout a building, insufficient communication networks can develop, resulting in role ambiguity and poor relationships. This problem is not restricted to offices. For example, one company found it had a high turnover and absenteeism among its assembly line workers, most of whom were women. When researchers looked into the problem, it was discovered that the women were isolated from one another owing to the layout of the conveyor belts used in the work. The women felt bored and lonely working without human interaction. Once the assembly line was reorganised to put the women into groups, absenteeism dropped substantially.

Shift work

Many workers today have jobs requiring them to work in shifts, some of which go round the clock. Many studies have found that shift work is a common occupational stressor. It has even been determined that shift work affects blood temperature, metabolic rate, blood sugar levels, mental efficiency and work motivation, not to mention sleep patterns and family and social life. In one study of air traffic controllers, shift work was isolated as a major problem, although other substantial job stressors were also present.[9] These workers had four times the prevalence of hypertension, and also more cases of mild diabetes and peptic ulcers, than did a control group of second-class airmen.

Long hours

The long working hours required in many jobs appear to take a toll on employee health. Studies have established a link between such hours and deaths due to coronary heart disease. In an investigation of light industrial workers in the USA it was found that individuals who were under 45 years of age and who worked more than 48 hours a week had twice the risk of death from coronary heart disease than did similar individuals working a maximum of 40 hours a week.[10] Another study of 100 young coronary patients revealed that 25 per cent of them had been working at two jobs and an additional 40 per cent worked for more than 60 hours a week.[11] Many individuals, such as executives working long hours and medical residents who may have no sleep for 36 hours or more, may find that both they and the quality of their work suffer. It is now commonly recognised that working beyond 40–50 hours a week results in time spent that is increasingly unproductive. Indeed, the EU Working Time Directive specifically limits member states to a 48-hour working week (with certain exceptions). However, it must be said that no large-scale systematic study has totally confirmed the detrimental effect of these hours; further research is needed.[12]

Travel

Although travel opportunities are appealing to many senior managers, travel can also be a source of stress. Traffic jams on the roads or at airports, delayed flights or trains, and the logistics of unknown places and people can present stressors as well as challenges. Marriages and families may suffer if one member spends significant periods of time away from home. In addition, a travelling manager spends less time with fellow workers and may miss out on opportunities or feel out of step with 'office politics'.

New technology

The introduction of new technology into the work environment has required management and workers alike to adapt continually to new equipment, systems and ways of working. Working under a boss trained in the 'old ways' may be an extra burden for a new employee trained in the latest methods and raises not only questions about the adequacy of supervision but also employee doubts about those in senior positions.

In a study investigating sources of stress among executives in 10 countries, Japanese executives suffered particularly from pressure to keep up with new technology, that is, to maintain their technological superiority.[13] Managers in developing countries felt pressure due to the increasing emphasis on new technology, the need to deal with an inadequately trained workforce and the imposition of deadlines. Also, in the UK, a high percentage (second only to Japan) of executives indicated that 'keeping up with new technology' was a great source of pressure at work. This is not surprising in a nation that, many people feel, is beginning to slip behind competitors in the race to grab new export markets. In addition, these UK managers describe a high level of stress due to the 'amount of travel' required by their work.

Work overload

Two different types of work overload have been described by researchers: 'quantitative' overload refers simply to having too much work to do, and 'qualitative' overload refers to work that is too difficult for an individual. In the first case, too much work often leads to working long hours, with the attendant problems described above. A too heavy work burden has also been connected with increased cigarette smoking, alcohol consumption and other stress indicators.[14]

A person's role in an organisation

When a person's role in an organisation is clearly defined and understood, and when expectations placed upon the individual are also clear and non-conflicting, stress can be kept to a minimum. But, as researchers have clearly seen, this is not the case in many places of work. Three critical factors – role ambiguity, role conflict and the degree of responsibility for others – are seen to be major sources of stress.[15]

Role ambiguity

Role ambiguity arises when an individual does not have a clear picture about work objectives, co-workers' expectations and the scope and responsibilities of the job. Often this ambiguity arises simply because a senior executive does not explain to the individual exactly what his or her role is. The stress indicators found to relate to role ambiguity are a depressed mood, lowered self-esteem, life dissatisfaction, low motivation to work and the intention to leave the job.

Role conflict

Role conflict exists when individuals are torn by conflicting job demands, or are doing things they do not really want to do, or things they do not believe are part of the job. Managers may often feel themselves torn between two groups of people who demand different types of behaviour or who believe the job entails different functions. As might be expected, studies have shown that people with high anxiety levels suffer more from role conflicts than do people who are more flexible in their approach to life.[16]

Responsibility

Responsibility has been found to be another organisational role stressor. In an organisation there are basically two types of responsibility: for people and for things (such as budgets, equipment and buildings). Responsibility for people has been found to be particularly stressful: studies in the 1960s revealed that this was far more likely to lead to coronary heart disease than was responsibility for things. Being responsible for people usually requires spending more time interacting with others, attending meetings and attempting to meet deadlines. An early investigation in the UK of 1,200 managers sent by their companies for annual medical examinations linked physical stress to age and level of responsibility.[17] The older the executive and the more responsibility held by the executive, the greater was the probability of coronary heart disease risk factors.

The stressful nature of having responsibility for others grew in the economic climate of the 1990s, a time when so many industries faced cost-cutting exercises. As industries implemented cutbacks in production and sales, managers were increasingly caught between the two goals of 'keeping personnel costs to a minimum' while also looking after the 'welfare of subordinates' in terms of job security and stability.

Relationships at work

Other people – and our varied encounters with them – can be major sources of either stress or support. At work, especially, dealings with bosses, peers and subordinates can dramatically affect the way we feel by the end of the day. Hans Selye has suggested that learning to live with other people is one of the most stressful aspects of life: 'good relationships between members of a group are a key factor in individual and organisational health.'[18]

There are three critical relationships at work: relationships with superiors, relationships with subordinates and relationships with colleagues or co-workers.

Relationships with superiors

Physicians and clinical psychologists support the idea that problems of emotional disability often result when the relationship between a subordinate and a boss is psychologically unhealthy for one reason or another. A US study of the relationship of workers to an immediate boss found that when the boss was perceived as considerate there was 'friendship, mutual trust, respect and a certain warmth between boss and subordinate'. Workers who said their boss was low on consideration reported feeling more job pressure. Workers who were under pressure reported that their bosses did not give them criticism in a helpful way, played favourites and 'pulled rank and took advantage of them whenever they had got a chance'.[19]

Relationships with subordinates

The way in which a manager supervises the work of others has always been considered a critical aspect of his or her work. For instance, an 'inability to delegate' has been a common criticism levelled against some managers. Managerial stress may be particularly high for those individuals with technical and scientific backgrounds, who may be more 'things-oriented'. For these managers, personal relationships may appear more trivial and time-consuming than for managers who are more 'people-oriented'. This is particularly true of individuals promoted, without management training, to management positions on the basis of their technical skills; they often encounter serious relationship problems at work.

Relationships with colleagues

Stress among co-workers may arise from the competition and personality conflicts usually described as 'office politics'. Adequate social support can be critical to the health and well-being of an individual and to the atmosphere and success of an organisation. Because most people spend so much time at work, the relationships among co-workers may provide valuable support or, conversely, be a huge source of stress.

A particular personality – that of the abrasive, hard-driving individual – has been seen to create stress for those around them. Harry Levinson of Harvard suggests that these abrasive people cause stress for other individuals because they ignore the interpersonal aspects of feelings and sensibilities of social interaction. The highly technical, achievement-oriented, hard-driving individual finds no time to consider working relationships and, as such, may be a source of interpersonal stress for others.

Career development

A host of issues can act as potential stressors throughout one's working life: lack of job security; fear of job loss; obsolescence or retirement; and numerous performance appraisals. In addition, the frustration of having reached one's career ceiling, or having been overpromoted, can result in extreme stress.

Job security

For many workers, career progression is of overriding importance – through promotion, people not only earn more money, but also receive increased status and new challenges. In the early years at a job, the striving and ability required to deal with a rapidly changing environment are usually rewarded by a company through financial and promotional rewards. In middle age, however, many people find their career progress has slowed or stopped. Job opportunities may become fewer, available jobs require longer to master, old knowledge becomes obsolete and energy levels flag at the same time that younger competition is threatening. The fear of demotion or obsolescence can be strong for those who believe they will suffer some erosion of status before they retire.

Job performance

The process of being evaluated and appraised can be a stressful experience for all of us. It must be recognised that performance appraisals can be anxiety-provoking, for both the individual being examined and the person doing the judging and appraising. The supervisor making performance judgements may face the threat of union grievance procedures in some cases, as well as interpersonal strains and the responsibility of making decisions affecting another person's livelihood.

The way in which an evaluation is carried out may affect the degree of anxiety experienced. For example, taking a written examination is a short-term stressor, whereas continuous and confidential appraisals by supervisors can have a longer-term effect, depending on the structure and climate of the organisation.

Organisational structure and climate

Just being part of an organisation can present threats to an individual's sense of freedom and autonomy. Organisational workers sometimes complain they do not have a sense of belonging, lack adequate opportunities to participate, feel their behaviour is unduly restricted and are not included in office communications and consultations.

As early as the 1940s researchers began reporting that workers who were allowed more participation in decision-making produced more and had higher job satisfaction.[20] In addition, researchers discovered that non-participation at work was a significant predictor of strain and job-related stress. It was found to be related to overall poor health, escapist drinking, depression, low self-esteem, absenteeism and plans to leave work.[21] Participation in the decision-making process on the part of individuals may help increase their feeling of investment in the company's success, create a sense of belonging and improve communication channels within the organisation. The resulting control, or sense of control, that participation provides seems vital for the well-being of all employees.[22]

Home/work pressures

Another danger of the current economic situation is the effect that work pressures (such as fear of job loss, blocked ambition, work overload and so on) have on the families of employees. At the very best of times, young managers, for example, face the inevitable conflict between organisational and family demands during the early build-up of their careers. But during an economic crisis, the problems increase in geometrical proportions, as individuals strive to cope with some of their basic economic and security needs. Under normal circumstances individuals find home a refuge from the competitive and demanding environment of work, a place where they can get support and comfort. However, when there is a career crisis (or stress from job insecurity), the tensions that individuals bring with them into the family affect the spouse and home environment in a way that may not meet their 'sanctuary' expectations. It may be very difficult, for example, for a wife to provide the kind of supportive domestic scene her husband requires at a time when she is beginning to feel insecure, or when she is worried about the family's economic, educational and social future.

It is difficult enough for a housebound wife to support her bread-winning husband and, at the same time, cope with family demands; but that stress is greater as, increasingly, women seek full-time careers themselves. According to the US Department of Labor, the 'typical American family' with a working husband, a homemaker wife and two children now makes up only 7 per cent of the nation's families. In fact, nearly 65 per cent of all women in the UK now work, more than half of them full-time. It is claimed by many psychologists and sociologists that dual-career family development is the primary culprit of the very large increase in the divorce rate over the last 10 years in the USA and Western European countries.

This dual-career culture of the family creates problems, particularly for women, because they are expected by men to work the 'double shift', in other words to pursue a job and also manage the home. Women, and society at large, are discovering the myth of the 'new man', who seems to exist only in the wishful thinking of women's magazine journalists! The dual-career family also creates problems for men. For example, many managers and executives are expected, as part of their job, to be mobile, that is, to be readily available for job transfers, both within and between countries. Indeed, promotional prospects may depend wholly on availability and willingness to accept promotional moves. In the late 1980s and 1990s, as women themselves began to pursue full-time careers (as opposed to part-time jobs), the prospects of professional men being available for rapid deployment fell substantially. In the past, these men have, with few exceptions, accepted promotional moves almost without family discussion. In the future such decisions will create major obstacles for both breadwinners in the family. We are already seeing this happen throughout Europe and the USA, and it is exacerbated particularly by the fact that corporations have not adapted to this changing social phenomenon. Few facilities are available in organisations to help either of the dual-career members of the family unit – facilities such as career-break schemes (eg the Barclays Bank scheme) or flexible working years.

The future stressors: the contract culture

In the early 1960s it was predicted by many social scientists and politicians that by 1990 we would all be working 20-hour weeks, with inordinate amounts of leisure time ensuring long lives and prosperity. New technology was going to be responsible for this leisure: computers and allied technological developments would transform our lives – would in effect 'take the strain', allowing us to pursue our grand dreams of cruising down the Norfolk Broads, walking in the Lake District, playing village cricket, gardening in the middle of the week and pursuing a whole range of activities forgotten in the 'enterprise culture' of the 1980s.

In reality, the immediate response demanded by new technology – by faxes, PCs, electronic mail and cellular phones – has been increased pressure. The pace of life has worsened, the stresses are greater and people are now working longer hours than they did in 1960: employees in general work about two to three hours a week longer, whereas in many cases managers work five to six hours longer. Indeed, the word 'stress' has found such a firm place in our modern vocabularies that we toss the term about casually to describe a wide range of 'aches and pains' resulting from our hectic pace of life. 'I really feel stressed out', someone says in order to describe a vague, yet often acute, sense of disquiet. 'She's under a lot of stress', we say when trying to understand a colleague's hyped-up behaviour or irritability. 'It's a high-stress job', someone says, awarding an odd sort of prestige to a fast-moving and overloaded occupation. But to those whose ability to cope with day-to-day matters is at crisis point the concept of stress is no longer a casual one. For them, the pace of life that creates stress can be translated into a four-letter word: pain.

In the first decade of the new millennium, the situation is likely to get worse. 'Leisure' will be a word consigned to the 'dustbin dictionary' of underused and underexperienced concepts. This period heralds enormous changes in the business world: in the increase in owner-managed companies; in efforts to retain our competitive position; in coping with EU regulations; in small businesses' developing strategic alliances and joint ventures with other similarly situated businesses; and all this coupled with the increasing pace of technological change in IT and methods of production and, most important of all, short-term contract working and increased teleworking.

These changes are happening against the backdrop of a two-earner family culture, as discussed above. This dual-career, or two-earner, family will exacerbate the stresses of life not only at home but also at work, because the home will no longer be the safe refuge many have been used to in the past. Weekends will be periods not of recovery and leisure activity but of doing the everyday things that could not be done during the week, or even be periods of working at home, as we are thrown onto our own resources as freelance workers. Many gloomy predictions have been made about the likely impact of the dual-career marriage on family members and the workplace. Sociologist Talcott Parsons has warned that such a lifestyle could throw a wife into destructive competition with her husband. If partners become adversaries rather than sources of mutual support, the situation will be fraught.

Yet in spite of these pessimistic appraisals, most recent researchers have concluded that the dual-career lifestyle has both costs and benefits.[23] The multiple demands of work and family without the support of a full-time helpmate can cause stress; but, equally, dual-careers provide the opportunity for multiple sources of satisfaction for both partners and wider access for industry to the pool of skills and talent, provided it can adapt to the changing structure of two-earner family life of the next millennium.

It should not be forgotten that the relationship between a traditional male breadwinner and a female homemaker can also be stressful to the individuals concerned. Generations of house-wives have suffered high rates of depression and lack of fulfil-ment. What Betty Friedan termed (in her book *The Feminine Mystique*), 'the problem with no name' is one consequence of a housewife role that fails to engage a person's skills. Similarly, the responsibilities of being the sole breadwinner can weigh heavily. The demands of the dual-career family are not neces-sarily greater than those of the traditional family; they are just different. It will be up to employers not only to understand this substantial social change in family life in the future and orient their human resource policies accordingly if work life is to be tolerable, but also to create the conditions for effective perfor-mance at work for the coming generations.

So what are the implications of all these trends for men and women and the organisations they work for? The increasingly flexible workplace of atypical working is no novelty for the grow-ing number of women entering paid employment, because women have always pursued discontinuous careers, working part-time or on short-term contracts as they managed both their careers and family life. Will this mean that men will become obsolete in this new contract culture, and that women will predominate because of their flexibility and ability to cope with insecurity and short-termism? If so, what impact will this have not only on corporate culture but also on responsibilities in the family or domestic arena? And, finally, how will organisations cope with this development? How long will they manage 'the commitment' of people to whom they are themselves no longer committed? How will they manage part-time or portfolio employees, people who are no longer motivated by the carrot-and-stick approach to promotion and career development? These questions of profound significance to the corporate world require careful consideration.[24]

No matter what else happens, the pace of change in the workplace and in organisations is likely to continue, forcing us to reflect on Lewis Carroll's observations in *Through the Looking-Glass*: 'A slow sort of country!' said the Queen. 'Now, here, you see, it takes all the running you can do, to keep in the same place. If you want to get somewhere else, you must run at least twice as fast as that.'

References

1 Cooper C. L. and Payne R. *Causes, Coping and Consequences of Stress at Work*. Chichester, John Wiley & Sons, 1988.

2 Cartwright S. and Cooper C. L. *No Hassle: Taking the stress out of work*. London, Century Books, 1994.

3 Cooper C. L. (ed.) *Handbook of Stress, Medicine and Health*. Boca Rotan, Florida, CRC Press, 1996.

4 Cooper C. L. and Quick J. C. *Stress and Strain*. Oxford, Health Press, 1999.

5 CBI. *Focus on Absence*. London, CBI, 2000.

6 Dale B. and Cooper C. L. *Total Quality and Human Resource Management*. Oxford, Blackwell, 1992.

7 Cooper C. and Smith M. *Job Stress and Blue-Collar Work*. Chichester, John Wiley & Sons, 1985.

8 Cobb S. and Rose R. H. 'Hypertension, peptic ulcer and diabetes in air traffic controllers'. *Journal of the Australian Medical Association*. 224. pp489–92. 1973.

9 Breslow L. and Buell P. 'Mortality from coronary heart disease and physical activity of work in California'. *Journal of Chronic Diseases*. II. pp615–24. 1975.

10 Russek H. I. and Zohman B. L. 'Relative significance of heredity, diet and occupational stress in CHD of young adults'. *American Journal of the Medical Sciences*. 253. pp266–75. 1958.

11 Harrington M. 'Working long hours and health'. *British Medical Journal*. 308. pp1581–2. 1994.

12 Cooper C. L. 'Executive stress: a ten-country comparison'. *Human Resource Management*. 23. pp395–407. 1984.

13 French J. R. P. and Caplan R. D. 'Organizational stress and individual strain', in A. J. Marrow (ed.), *The Failure of Success*, New York, AMACOM, pp30–60, 1972.

14 Ivancevich J. M. and Matteson M. T. *Stress and Work*. Illinois, Scott, Foresman and Company, 1980.

15 Quick J. C. and Quick J. D. *Organizational Stress and Preventive Management*. New York, McGraw-Hill, 1984.

16 Pincherle A. 'Fitness for work'. *Proceedings of the Royal Society of Medicine*. 65. pp321–4. 1972.

17 Selye H. 'The General Adaptation Syndrome and the diseases of adaptation'. *Journal of Clinical Endocrinology*. VI. p117. 1946.

18 Buck V. *Working Under Pressure*. London, Staples Press, 1972.

19 Coch L. and French J. R. P. 'Overcoming resistance to change'. *Human Relations*. I. pp512–32. 1948.

20 Margolis B., Kroes W. and Quinn R. 'Job stress: an unlisted occupational hazard'. *Journal of Occupational Medicine*. 16, 10. pp654–61. 1974.

21 Sutherland V. and Cooper C. L. *Strategic Stress Management*. London, Macmillan Press, 2000.

22 Cooper C. L. and Lewis S. *Balancing your Career, Family and Life*. London, Kogan Page, 1998.

23 Cooper C. L. and Jackson S. *Creating Tomorrow's Organizations*. Chichester and New York, John Wiley & Sons, 1998.

24 Cooper C. L. 'The changing psychological contract at work'. *European Business Journal*. 11, 3. pp115–19. 1999.

4 PERSONAL INJURY ACTIONS BASED ON WORKPLACE STRESS

Introduction and historical setting

Most employers have been aware for many years that they may be sued by employees who are injured at work or who contract a work-related disease. If a court finds the employer to have been negligent in failing to prevent the injury, the employee is entitled to compensation, and since 1969 the law has required the employer to be insured against such claims (Employers' Liability (Compulsory Insurance) Act 1969). What had not crossed employers' minds until more recently was the possibility of such a personal injury claim being brought where their employee had suffered a stress-induced illness, perhaps more correctly described as a psychiatric injury.

Personal injury actions are based on common law, ie they arise out of the law as developed by the decisions of judges over the years rather than by legislation in the form of Acts of Parliament. During the nineteenth century two strands of legal development were particularly relevant in shaping the law in this area. The first was the slowly changing attitude of the courts to the question of whether employers should be held responsible for the safety of their workforce; the second was the emerging law of negligence based on the notion of a duty of care owed by one person to another. By 1937 it was established, in the case of *Wilsons & Clyde Coal Company Limited* v *English*,[1] that employers owed a duty of care to their employees. In the course of the judgment Lord Wright stated:

> The whole course of authority consistently recognises a duty which rests on the employer, and which is personal to the employer, to take reasonable care for the safety of his workmen.

The case is generally regarded as the foundation of the modern law of employers' liability, in that they would be liable to compensate employees if they broke the duty by negligent conduct. Failure to take reasonable care for an employee's safety can also be seen as a breach of contract, because it is now accepted that the duty of care takes effect as an implied term in the contract of employment.

The common law thus established that employees fell generally within a category of recognised legal duty. However, a more relevant question to ask is: against what types of harm does the employer's duty to protect employees extend? More specifically, is the employer under a duty to protect the workforce against psychiatric harm?

In the past, the issue of psychiatric harm at work has arisen in two main ways. First, there have been instances in which employees who suffered a physical injury also experienced psychological symptoms consequent upon the physical injury. To take an example, suppose a worker is injured by a heavy object falling on his foot. His period of absence from work is extended because, at a time when his physical injury has healed, he believes himself unable to work. Such a condition (known as functional overlay) has not presented the courts with a legal difficulty; provided they were satisfied with the validity of the claim, they have been willing to compensate the injured worker for the entire period of absence. Secondly, there have been a limited number of what are commonly termed 'nervous shock' cases, in which psychiatric harm has been caused by some traumatic event. They have not, in general, focused on workplace incidents, and therefore the law in this area has not developed with the employer-employee relationship in mind. However, as violence in modern society has increased, a growing number of employees, for example in banks, building societies and the retail sector, are being subjected to traumatic incidents leading to symptoms of stress. Further discussion of the duty of care in 'nervous shock' cases is therefore given on pages 41–42 below.

The novel issue brought to the fore in the landmark case of

Walker v *Northumberland County Council*[2] was what attitude the courts would take to the question of the employer's duty to protect against psychiatric harm generally. The judge's view was that:

> Whereas the law on the extent of this duty has developed almost exclusively in cases involving physical injury to the employee as distinct from injury to his mental health, there is no logical reason why risk of psychiatric damage should be excluded from the scope of the duty of care.

By embracing psychiatric damage within employers' legal duty to their workforce, this case and the judicial views expressed in it are crucial to organisations feeling their way in a new situation of potential legal liability. The facts of the case are therefore presented here in some detail, and the legal issues are discussed by frequent reference to them as well as to other relevant decided cases.

The John Walker case: the facts

Mr Walker worked for Northumberland County Council from 1970 until December 1987 as an area social services officer. His was a middle-management position, and he was responsible for four teams of social services fieldworkers in the Blyth Valley area of Northumberland. This area had a relatively high incidence of childcare problems, in particular those relating to allegations of child abuse. Mr Walker was responsible for the manning of these cases by his teams of field social workers and for the holding of case conferences in respect of children referred to his area of the Social Services Department. During the 1980s the population of Blyth Valley rose, leading to an increase in the volume of work to be undertaken by Mr Walker and his teams, but there was no corresponding rise in the number of fieldworkers. Mr Walker and his team were increasingly under pressure, and this, of itself and apart from the stressful nature of the work, created stress and anxiety.

Between 1985 and 1987 Mr Walker repeatedly complained (in writing) to his superiors, expressing the need to alleviate the work pressure to which he and his social workers were subject. Recognising that the council would be unwilling to approve increased resources, Mr Walker requested instead a redistribution of resources from rural areas to urban areas such as his own. In November 1985 Mr Walker told his superior, Mr Davidson, that the Blyth Valley area should be split in two, and that he did not think he could go on shouldering his then volume of work. Mr Davidson told Mr Walker he was unwilling to make changes at that point, because within two years there was to be a restructuring of social services in the county. Mr Walker indicated that in that case he could go on, but he could not go beyond two years. During 1986 the workload continued to increase and in November 1986 Mr Walker suffered a nervous breakdown.

On 4 March 1987 Mr Walker returned to work, having negotiated for assistance to be provided for him on his return. As things turned out, support was provided to Mr Walker on an intermittent basis only and was withdrawn by early April. During his absence a substantial backlog of paperwork had built up, which took Mr Walker till May to clear. In the meantime the number of pending cases continued to increase and Mr Walker began to experience stress symptoms once again. By 16 September 1987 he was advised to go on sick leave and was diagnosed as being affected by a state of stress-related anxiety. In the event, he suffered a second mental breakdown and was obliged to retire from his post for reasons of ill-health.

The judge, Colman J., held that the council was liable for Mr Walker's second nervous breakdown, but not for his first.

The legal issues

The need to suffer an 'injury'

It is self-evident that in personal injury cases based on the tort[3] of negligence the plaintiff must have actually suffered an injury. In a typical case this would have occurred as a result of an accident such as an explosion, slipping, being splashed with toxic materials or being trapped in machinery. 'Injury' has also encompassed industrial diseases such as asbestosis, pneumoconiosis and noise-induced deafness. However, in the context of actions based on workplace stress, it is important to realise that merely to suffer from 'stress' is unlikely to be sufficient to found a claim. In a recent Scottish case,[4] it was emphasised that the plaintiff employee will have to establish that he or she was suffering from a recognised psychiatric illness (or a physical illness recognised to have psychological origins). This would normally be done by reference to one or other of the main diagnostic classificatory systems of mental disorders used by the psychiatric profession:

- the American Diagnostic and Statistical Manual of Mental Disorders (DSM-IV)
- the International Classification of Diseases and Related Health Problems (ICD-10, which also covers physical conditions).

Although a detailed discussion of psychiatric illness as described in DSM-IV and ICD-10 is outside the scope of this book, mental disorders can be broadly classified as follows:

Personality disorders

These are due neither to mental illness nor to intellectual impairment, but rather to abnormal development from childhood, eg hysterical or obsessional personalities. Although personality disorders are thus not themselves caused by workplace stress, they may be relevant in that context because a person with a pre-existing personality disorder who is subjected to stress or trauma may suffer a disproportionate reaction to it (see the 'egg-shell skull rule' discussed on pages 46–7 below).

Mental impairment

This is characterised as a learning disability and is of little relevance for our purposes, because it is not environmentally caused.

Psychoses

These are serious mental disorders, which can be subdivided further into organic psychoses and functional psychoses. The former are caused by physical damage to the brain or nervous system, and hence may be part and parcel of a 'normal' personal injury claim. Functional psychoses are severe disorders such as schizophrenia, that lack a physical cause. They are difficult to define but are said to be characterised by a loss of touch with reality on the part of the sufferer.

Neuroses

These are generally less serious than psychoses, and include such conditions as anxiety disorders, phobic disorders, certain types of depression and obsessional neuroses. It is recognised that neuroses can be caused by distressing experiences, and they are therefore likely to be the chief focus of interest in legal claims arising out of workplace stress.

There are also other disorders such as sexual dysfunction, and those attributed to drugs or alcohol dependence.

Stress-related neuroses

The neuroses most likely to be stress-related are anxiety disorders and mood disorders, particularly those of a depressive nature; these are outlined in considerable detail in the two diagnostic classification systems. Although Mr Walker is described as having suffered a nervous breakdown, his actual diagnosis was 'stress-related anxiety state' and 'chronic anxiety state with acute exacerbations and the presence at times of reactive depressive symptoms'.

Depression

This is a term in common usage, and can mean anything from a major illness to mild feelings of being 'fed-up'. In DSM-IV depressive disorders are listed as subclassifications of mood disorders, and range from major depressive episodes to less severe conditions. They are characterised by depressed mood (feeling sad or 'down in the dumps'), a loss of interest or pleasure in normal activities, and a range of other common symptoms, including:

☐ diminished appetite and weight loss
☐ insomnia
☐ diminished ability to concentrate, or indecisiveness
☐ thoughts of death, plans to commit suicide, or suicide attempts (up to 15 per cent of those suffering major depressive disorder die by suicide)
☐ fatigue without physical exertion, and loss of energy
☐ feelings of guilt and self-worthlessness.

Anxiety disorders

Neither ICD-10 nor DSM-IV gives an overall description of anxiety disorders, but ICD-9 (ie an earlier version) states that they are:

> various combinations of physical and mental manifestations of anxiety, not attributable to real danger and occurring either in attacks or as a persisting state. The anxiety is usually diffuse and may extend to panic. Other neurotic features such as obsessional or hysterical symptoms may be present but do not dominate the clinical picture.

Panic attacks are periods during which the person experiences intense fear or discomfort, accompanied by a number (at least four) of the following symptoms:

- □ palpitations
- □ sweating
- □ trembling or shaking
- □ breathlessness
- □ a feeling of choking
- □ chest pain or discomfort
- □ nausea
- □ dizziness or light-headedness
- □ feelings of unreality or being detached from oneself
- □ fear of losing control or going crazy
- □ fear of dying
- □ numbness or tingling sensations
- □ chills or hot flushes.

It is also recognised that physical conditions associated with stress, such as headaches or irritable bowel syndrome, often accompany anxiety disorder.

Post-traumatic stress disorder (PTSD)

PTSD is the nearest modern equivalent to the old-fashioned-sounding 'nervous shock'. It has come to the forefront through such disasters as those at Zeebrugge and Hillsborough, and is likely to become important in terms of potential litigation because employees in, for example, the retail sector or in public services are increasingly exposed to violent incidents during their working lives. A survey by the Banking, Insurance and Finance Union (BIFU) revealed that in 1991 there were 1,633 raids on banks and building societies; almost every case involved the use of a weapon or threats of violence.[5] Such raids result in traumatised staff with poor morale and significantly reduced effectiveness, and research suggests that 25 per cent of individuals who experience PTSD in this way suffer long-term effects.[6]

According to the ICD-10, the main feature of the disorder is 'the development of characteristic symptoms following a psychologically distressing event or situation of an exceptionally threatening or catastrophic nature'.[7] DSM-IV lists two necessary vital characteristics of the initiating event in order for a diagnosis of PTSD to be made. These are:

☐ that the person in question experienced, witnessed, or was confronted with an event or events that involved actual or threatened death or serious injury, or a threat to the physical integrity of self or others

☐ that his or her response involved intense fear, helplessness, or horror.[8]

Symptoms of PTSD typically include persistent re-experience of the event, for example through dreams, and intense distress when exposed to events that symbolise or resemble an aspect of the original incident. Sufferers also experience irritability, difficulty in concentrating and sleep disturbance; they also avoid anything that reminds them of the event (see Appendix 2 for more detail).

Although PTSD is generally thought to set in following a single traumatic event, it appears that PTSD-like symptoms can also be produced by a sequence of less intense events over a period of time. The onset of these symptoms following prolonged duress is sometimes referred to as Prolonged Duress Stress Disorder, and may be particularly relevant in cases of bullying at work (see Chapter 6).

The duty of care

The duty to protect against psychiatric harm

The judge in John Walker's case set out the basic proposition in relation to the duty of care. He said:

> It is now clear law that an employer has a duty to provide his employee with a reasonably safe system of work and to take reasonable steps to protect him from *risks which are reasonably foreseeable*.

The first question was, therefore, whether the council could have foreseen at the time of his first breakdown that Mr Walker was at risk of damage to his mental health. The judge dealt with this matter in two parts:

- ☐ Should anything have alerted the council to the fact that its area officers in *general* (or others in middle management in Social Services) were at risk of mental illness? The answer to this was no, because there was a lack of evidence that the council had previously encountered mental illness in any of its workers in those positions.
- ☐ Should the council have foreseen that *Mr Walker* was exposed to a higher risk of mental illness than that affecting others in his position with a heavy workload?

The answer to this was also in the negative, because although Mr Walker had complained about the excessive workload and asked for something to be done about it, he had not conveyed to his superior, Mr Davidson, that his health was likely to be affected if no such steps were taken. Mr Walker's assertion that he could not see himself going on beyond two years was seen as a statement relating to his ability to provide effective management rather than an indication of the approach of mental breaking point.

The point about looking at employees as individuals and at the facts known about them is important, because this was the reason why the plaintiff in an earlier case (*Petch* v *Customs and Excise Commission*)[9] was unsuccessful. Mr Petch suffered a mental breakdown caused, at least partially, by work pressures, but the judge found that, until his breakdown, the plaintiff

> showed himself not only able to cope with the existing workload but enthusiastic to take on more . . . It seems to me that the plaintiff revelled in his work and enjoyed every minute of it.

Witnesses testified that he was the last person they would have expected to break down under the pressures of work.

In contrast, the judge found that, when Mr Walker resumed work after his first breakdown, Mr Davidson should have appreciated that Mr Walker was more vulnerable to psychiatric harm than he had previously appeared to be, and should have foreseen that if Mr Walker was exposed once again to the same workload there was a risk of his suffering a similar mental illness.

Can the duty be overridden by the express terms of the contract of employment?

In addition to the implied terms in a contract of employment relating, for instance, to the employer's duty of care or to the duty of good faith, there are also likely to be a number of express terms setting out such things as hours of work, the rate of pay, the place of work and job duties. Whereas in the normal course of events the express and implied terms coexist or complement each other, there are occasions when there is in fact potential conflict between them.

The issue can be conveniently considered by examining the case of *Johnstone* v *Bloomsbury Health Authority*.[10] Chris Johnstone was a senior house officer whose contract of employment required him to work a basic 40-hour week and to be available on call for up to a further 48 hours' overtime. He alleged that, as a result of working excessively long hours, he suffered symptoms of stress and depression manifested through difficulty in eating and sleeping, by occasionally being physically sick from exhaustion, and by frequently experiencing suicidal feelings. In addition to claiming damages, he sought a declaration that he could not be required to work 'for so many hours in excess of his standard working week as would foreseeably injure his health', even if this was less than the 48 hours' availability stipulated in his contract. In essence, the issue was whether the implied term of his contract that the health authority would take reasonable care for his health and safety took precedence over the express provision to work up to 88 hours in total.

A lawyer's response to such a question would in general be that the scope of an express term cannot normally be cut down by an implied term. However, that was not the unanimous opinion of the three Court of Appeal (CA) judges hearing the case. In fact, each judge took a different stance. In the view of the first, the duty of care could not be overridden by the express terms of the contract. The power to require Mr Johnstone to work up to 88 hours a week had to be exercised in the light of the duty to take care for his safety. Drawing a parallel with cases of physical injury, he stated:

> If these were the hours of a contract of a heavy goods driver, and he fell asleep at the wheel through exhaustion and suffered injury, I entertain no doubt that...the employee would have a good claim against his employer for operating an unsafe system of work.

The second judge disagreed in part. He accepted that the absolute duty to work 40 hours a week could not be cut down by the implied duty of care but felt that, because the health authority had a discretion in respect of the additional overtime hours, they should not exercise that discretion in a way that injured the employee's health. The final judge regarded this distinction between contracted hours and hours to be available on call to be unwarranted, and he pointed to the difficulty for the authority in having to assess the number of hours that could be required of individual doctors, each with a varying degree of physical stamina. In the judge's view, Mr Johnstone had contracted to make himself available for 88 hours, and that express term could not be cut down by an implied term.

Whereas the judges were thus at variance over the issue of the supremacy of the express terms, they were nevertheless in agreement that if the express terms of the contract were to prevail, they would arguably be rendered ineffective by S2(1) of the Unfair Contract Terms Act 1977. This provides that:

> a person cannot by reference to any contract term...exclude or restrict his liability for . . . personal injury resulting from negligence.

The Act is more normally applicable to the sort of standard exclusion clauses (that the company is not liable if accidents occur) formerly to be found on car-parking tickets and the like, but it was accepted by the Court that if the express obligation to work up to 88 hours prevented Chris Johnstone from bringing a claim in negligence based on breach of the duty of care, then in substance, if not in form, it was indeed a contract term restricting the authority's liability for personal injury.

This hearing in the Court of Appeal in 1991 was merely an unsuccessful application by the authority to have the claim thrown out without its proceeding to trial. Much interest centred not only on what the final legal outcome would be but also on the implications for the working conditions of hospital doctors throughout the UK. Some four years later, very shortly before the trial of the main action was due to begin, the claim was settled for £5,600 and payment of costs. No doubt Chris Johnstone regarded this as a moral victory, but the lack of a ruling leaves the law in a most undesirable state of uncertainty on what is clearly an important issue for cases involving working hours.

The duty to employees with a particular sensitivity – 'the egg-shell skull rule'

If an employer can foresee that there is a risk to the mental health of a class of employees or to a given individual, liability cannot be avoided on the basis that the extent of the injury to the particular individual was not foreseeable. In other words, employers must take their victims as they find them.

For example, in a non-employment case (*Brice* v *Brown*)[11] a woman with a pre-existing underlying personality disorder was involved in a road traffic accident in which her daughter was, it appeared, badly injured. It was foreseeable that she would suffer some 'nervous shock', but in fact she experienced a hysterical reaction to the stress, which resulted in a severe mental illness. The judge found that she was entitled to damages for her condition, which included the cost of having someone to care for her, even though the defendant could not have foreseen that she would react so badly to the situation.

It should be emphasised, however, that if the employee were to suffer psychiatric damage because of a particular susceptibility, but the employer could not have foreseen this type of harm at all, there will be no liability. Thus, in the case of John Walker it was successfully argued that the council was not liable for his first nervous breakdown because it was not foreseeable that social workers in his position were at risk of psychiatric harm. John Walker's breakdown was simply caused by his own particular susceptibility. Nevertheless, once employers are put on notice that a given individual is susceptible to psychiatric harm, they will be liable if it is foreseeable in the circumstances that that individual will suffer such harm. Hence the council's liability for Mr Walker's second breakdown.

The duty in 'nervous shock' cases

Most of the existing 'nervous shock' cases are, as stated earlier, non-employment cases, and the law surrounding them has recently been reviewed.[12] Partly on account of a scepticism (at least historically) about the validity of claims of 'nervous shock' and the ease with which they could be fabricated, and partly because of the fear of a multiplicity of claims, mere foreseeability of the risk of psychiatric harm has not been sufficient to give rise to a duty of care. The courts have restricted liability by means of 'control mechanisms' – in other words, more or less arbitrary conditions which plaintiffs must satisfy. The 'rules' about when a duty will arise were drawn together in the case of *Alcock* v *Chief Constable of S. Yorks*,[13] in which relatives of the Hillsborough disaster victims sought compensation. They were then clarified and modified somewhat in a subsequent case, *White* v *Chief Constable of S. Yorks*,[14] in which police officers who were on duty that day claimed to have suffered psychiatric injury by reason of their involvement in the horrifying events. The tragedy arose when police allowed football fans to enter pens that were already overcrowded with supporters. In the ensuing crush of bodies and the struggle by fans to get out of the pens, 95 people were killed and over 400 physically injured. The judgments of the House of Lords in the two cases appear to mean that:

- □ a duty will arise only if (in addition to psychiatric harm being foreseeable to a person of reasonable fortitude) the plaintiff objectively exposed himself or herself to danger or reasonably believed that he or she was doing so, eg a man living near the scene of a serious train crash who assisted for several hours and who suffered an adverse psychiatric reaction (*Chadwick* v *British Railways Board*)[15], or
  — although not personally imperilled, witnessed the trauma or arrived on the scene shortly afterwards (ie perceived

the immediate aftermath) and had a sufficiently 'proximate' relationship to the victim, eg parent-child, spouse, fiancé(e), or

— was a so-called 'conduit pipe', in that, as a result of the defendant's negligence, he or she was put in the position of believing that he or she was about to be, or had been, the cause of another's death or injury, and suffers shock-induced illness in consequence (for an example, see the case of *Dooley* v *Cammell Laird & Co. Ltd*[16] below)

☐ mere 'bystanders' are normally excluded, including those who are simply told of a traumatic event or watch it on the television. It should be noted that only one of the 16 relatives in the *Alcock* case fulfilled the requirements of the above point. The rest were regarded as bystanders and lost their cases. The House of Lords in the *Alcock* case did suggest that '[A bystander] could not perhaps be entirely excluded . . . if the circumstances of a catastrophe occurring very close to him were particularly horrific', but if that is so it is difficult to conceive of an incident more horrific than that which occurred at Hillsborough.

☐ damages are recoverable only in respect of a recognised psychiatric illness. Grief, distress and anxiety are not sufficient.

☐ where shock causes physical injury, damages are recoverable, as for any other personal injury.

It follows logically from these principles that retail assistants, for example, or those working in banks or building societies who are involved in a hold-up and suffer PTSD through fear for their own safety, should not be excluded.

However, employees who are not personally imperilled are likely to be excluded on the grounds that they are mere bystanders, even though it is foreseeable that they may suffer a shock-induced illness by witnessing their working colleagues imperilled. This limitation was confirmed in the Scottish case of *Robertson and Rough* v *Forth Road Bridge Joint Board*.[17] The two plaintiffs were working on the Forth Road Bridge with their colleague, Mr Smith; he, owing to a sudden and violent gust of wind, was thrown off the back of Mr Rough's pick-up truck, in which he had been sitting while the truck was travelling across the bridge. Mr Robertson, who was following behind in another vehicle, witnessed what happened and subsequently saw Mr Smith fall over the side of the bridge to his death on a girder below the carriageway. Mr Rough heard a bang and immediately got out to see what had happened. Mr Robertson and Mr Rough's claims for damages for nervous shock resulting in psychiatric injuries failed, the court ruling that:

> where the employees are merely bystanders or witnesses, the ordinary rule must apply. They must be assumed to be possessed of sufficient fortitude to enable them to endure the shock caused by witnessing accidents to their fellow employees.

The argument that the relationship of employer and employee should of itself bring the plaintiffs within this sort of duty of care was specifically rejected[18] (even though the court accepted that the requirement for such a relationship would reduce the risk of large numbers of claims). Nor could the plaintiffs assert that they had believed themselves to be the cause of Mr Smith's death and thus bring themselves within the 'conduit pipe' category of duty. In the employment context, an early example of this type of case is that of *Dooley* v *Cammell Laird & Co. Ltd* (see note 16), in which a crane driver working in a shipyard successfully sued his employer. He suffered nervous shock after the sling to the fall of his crane broke, whereupon the load fell into the hold of the ship where he knew his fellow workers were loading. Three similar cases involve railway workers:

☐ *Galt* v *British Railways Board*,[19] in which a train driver rounded a bend and came upon two railwaymen. It was impossible for him to stop, and he believed the two men had been killed by his train.

☐ *Wigg* v *British Railways Board*,[20] where a train driver came upon the body of a person very soon after it had been struck by the door of the train he was driving as it pulled out from a station.

☐ *Dillon* v *British Railways Board*,[21] in which a train that had proceeded beyond a red signal collided with another train on the same track as a result of the operation of the signal by the plaintiff signalman.

Until recently it was generally accepted that there was a further category of persons, known as 'rescuers', who would not be subject to the 'control mechanisms' set out in the *Alcock* case and discussed on pages 47–8. These were persons such as the plaintiff in *Chadwick* v *British Railways Board* (note 15) who became involved in a dangerous situation caused by the negligence of the defendant and were themselves injured in rescuing others. However, the legal position of professional rescuers was complicated and somewhat unsatisfactory. Previously, professional rescuers such as firemen or the police had not been prevented from successfully bringing claims based on physical injury, solely on the basis that such injury was a risk inherent in their occupation (see the discussion below of *volenti*, pages 56–7). However, in the case of psychiatric harm the situation was less clear. Liability was admitted by the defendant in the case of a fireman who suffered PTSD as a result of his involvement in the King's Cross Fire (*Hale* v *London Underground Limited*),[22] and 14 police officers who went into the pens in which fans were crushed to death at Hillsborough reached out-of-court settlements with their employer. However, the High Court subsequently ruled against six other police officers on duty that day (*Frost and Others* v *Chief Constable of S. Yorks and Others*).[23] The judge held that either they were not sufficiently involved in the immediate aftermath to be classed as rescuers or, even if they were, it was not 'fair and reasonable' to allow them to recover when spectators who would be less likely to be hardened to such incidents could not (because they were regarded as mere bystanders). The House of Lords (in the case of *White* v *Chief Constable of S. Yorks* referred to on page 47) have now denied that there is a specific category of 'rescuers' as opposed to persons who expose themselves to physical danger. For this reason the police who assisted in the aftermath of the Hillsborough disaster failed in their claims because, although they suffered psychiatric injury following their involvement, it was generally accepted that they were not exposed to physical danger.

Breach of duty

Whether or not the defendant has breached the duty of care involves an examination of what would be a reasonable response to avoid the risk of foreseeable harm. The result is a balancing exercise and if, for example, the risk of harm is remote, it may be reasonable to do nothing about it.

The following factors must be considered:

□ the likelihood of psychiatric harm, and its gravity
□ the cost and practicability of preventing the risk
□ the state of knowledge
□ the 'usefulness' of the acts alleged to be in breach of duty
□ reasonableness in the circumstances.

There is also the question of vicarious liability. We shall examine each of these factors in turn.

The likelihood of psychiatric harm, and its gravity

In the case of John Walker, the judge concluded that in respect of his first breakdown the risk of mental breakdown was not substantial enough to cause the council to be under a duty in respect of it. However, when Mr Walker returned to work after his breakdown, the risk of repetition and the seriousness of a second breakdown did require the council to act.

Employers need therefore to know the answers to the following questions:

□ What are the risks in general to the mental health of this *group* of workers, eg area social services officers or building society managers, and what is the *degree* of risk?
□ Is there anything I know, or *should* know, about this individual that makes it more (or less!) likely that he or she is at risk?
□ Is there anything to indicate to me *how serious* any ensuing harm is likely to be (either to a group or to an individual)?

The cost and practicability of preventing the risk

The issue is summed up neatly in the House of Lords case of *Latimer* v *AEC Limited*,[24] namely:

> in every case of foreseeable risk it is a matter of balancing the risk against the measures necessary to eliminate it.

In Mr Walker's case, the judge found that the only course of action that would have had a reasonable chance of preventing

Mr Walker's having a second nervous breakdown would have been to have provided continuous, or at least substantial, back-up for Mr Walker in his Blyth office. In examining the practicability of such a course of action the judge then explored the staffing problems of the council. He found that there was no surplus staff capacity and that, in consequence, substantial assistance to Mr Walker could have been provided only at the expense of some disruption to other social work. Nonetheless, given the size of the risk of repetition of Mr Walker's illness, that measure of assistance should have been provided, had the local authority been acting reasonably, despite the possible disruptive effect on the council's provision of services to the public.

Employers may therefore need to consider such questions as these:

☐ What extra resources, and at what cost, may I need to provide in order to reduce an employee's workload?

☐ Would management training be effective in reducing the risks of bullying and harassment?

☐ Are security measures appropriate to protect staff from violent attacks?

The state of knowledge

In cases of negligence, the defendant is judged in the light of the expert knowledge available at the time of the alleged breach of duty. In the past, little was known about the psychiatric harm that could be caused by events in the workplace, but increasingly the sources of stress at work and its consequences are being researched. Guidelines from the Health and Safety Executive (HSE) have now put workplace stress firmly on the map as a health and safety issue (see Chapter 5). Employers who are ignorant about knowledge that is available will not be able to shelter behind their failure to acquaint themselves with the facts.

The 'usefulness' of the acts alleged to be in breach of duty

In physical injury cases, the purpose served by the defendant's acts would occasionally justify the assumption of a risk that would otherwise be objectionable. For example, driving manoeuvres in wartime or during emergency services might be held reasonable when in normal circumstances they would not. It will be interesting to see whether, as case law develops on psychiatric harm, the reverse will be true – whether, in other words, where acts are done with an improper motive, such as to harass employees or to drive them out, the behaviour will be regarded as unreasonable or, if it is done to improve performance or tide the organisation through a difficult time, it will be tolerated.

Reasonableness in the circumstances

It must be stressed that the law requires only a reasonable response. It does not require employers to remove all risks to health and safety at whatever cost. There may be, for example, risks inherent to the job (although employers who fail to warn employees of the risks may be acting unreasonably – see Chapter 7).

Remember: An employer is negligent only by failing to do what is reasonable in the circumstances, or by doing what is not reasonable. The plaintiff must prove the employer to be at fault.

Vicarious liability

If an employee suffers injury through the negligence (or other tortious act) of a fellow employee acting in the course of employment, the employer will be vicariously liable for the wrong-doing of that employee. Although in theory there is nothing to prevent the injured employee suing the individual who inflicted the harm, in practice it will be the employer against whom action will be taken. The most obvious reason for this is, as noted earlier, the requirement for the employer to be insured against personal injury claims.

In the case of Mr Walker, vicarious liability was not an issue raised, it being regarded as the council's own negligence to fail to provide him with support, rather than the council's being made liable for the unreasonable behaviour of, for example, Mr Davidson, Mr Walker's superior. It is likely that this will be the way in which cases based on long working hours or overwork will generally be run. However, this may not be so in litigation arising out of bullying, in which a specific individual can be pointed to as causing the harm. In such cases there may indeed be an issue as to whether the individual was acting in the course of employment or 'on a frolic of his own' – in which case the employer would not be liable. If an employee performs an act expressly or implicitly authorised by the employer, it is normally accepted that he or she is acting in the course of employment. Where the individual's behaviour is wrongful or prohibited by the employer, the 'rule' is that:

☐ doing an authorised act in an unauthorised manner is held to be in the course of employment

☐ doing an unauthorised act, or one outside the scope of that individual's job, is not held to be in the course of employment.

Although this distinction is easy to state (if notoriously difficult to apply), it is likely that bullying or generalised harassment by managers of their subordinates would be regarded as being in the course of employment. It should also be noted that where a claim of sexual or racial harassment is brought in an employment tribunal, the phrase 'in the course of employment' should not be construed in this way (see Chapter 5).

Injury caused by the breach of duty

The plaintiff in a personal injury case must prove that the employer's breach did one or other of the following:

☐ it caused the injury

☐ it materially increased the risk of injury.

In situations where it is alleged that workplace stress was the cause of the injury, there are likely to be real problems surrounding the issue of causation, because many people also have stresses and strains outside the workplace such as financial worries or problems with personal relationships, and it may be difficult to disentangle the various pressures to which a given individual is subject. In addition, there are physical conditions such as heart attacks and strokes that may well be stress-related but that may equally be caused by non-stress triggers such as diet, smoking, 'Type A' behaviour or genetic predisposition.

Medical evidence in stress cases will therefore be crucial. Mr Walker's expert witness testified that his personality was normal in the sense that he suffered from no personality abnormality, and submitted that Mr Walker's breakdown was due to:

- □ the mounting and quite uncontrollable workload
- □ feelings of responsibility for the young children under the care of his field teams
- □ feelings of responsibility for the overworked field teams in his area
- □ a feeling of frustrated helplessness because he found himself in a deteriorating situation that he was powerless to control.

The judge accepted that Mr Walker's breakdown was caused by his working environment. He found that:

> the stress created by his determination to provide the required services without unduly overloading his field teams and by his inability to persuade the Council to support him placed him . . . in a position where he was trapped between the two problems.

In effect, the council's failure to provide Mr Walker with sufficient resources drove him to the point of despair.

Whereas the causation requirement will be easier to satisfy in the case of a normal personality, an underlying predisposition to mental illness will not necessarily cause a claim to fail. In the Petch case (see page 43), the plaintiff, who was a manic depressive, suffered a nervous breakdown. However, the judge was not satisfied he would have suffered the breakdown even without being subjected to the pressure of work. The crucial question appears to be this: would this person have suffered psychiatric harm but for the pressure of work (or whatever is alleged to be the employer's breach of duty)?

An Australian case, *Gillespie* v *Commonwealth of Australia*,[25] provides further illustration of the point. A former diplomat had been posted to Caracas, Venezuela, and claimed that the stressful living conditions had resulted in his suffering a breakdown. He submitted that the defendants should have prepared him for these stressful conditions by sending him on a training course before he went to Venezuela. However, the judge was not persuaded that if Mr Gillespie had been warned he would either not have gone to Caracas at all or (had he still decided to go) avoided the mental breakdown. Hence it was not established that the alleged breach of duty (the failure to warn about the conditions) had caused the injury, and the plaintiff lost the case.

Defences

Consent to the risk of harm (volenti)

The legal doctrine of *volenti non fit injuria* ('to one who is willing, no harm is done') means that it is a defence to a claim in negligence if the plaintiff both knew of the risks of injury and consented to run the risks of the defendant's negligence. This defence has been successfully raised in the case of spectators attending sporting activities. One case involved a boy who was injured at an ice-hockey match when the puck was hit out of the rink; in another, a photographer was injured by a horse during a jumping show.

However, in employment situations the courts have been less ready to accept the defence, generally because employees may well be aware of the risks but can rarely be said truly to consent to run them. Moreover, what must be shown is that the employee consented to run the risk of the *employer's negligence*, not merely the *inherent risks* of the job. This is not to say that the defence could never apply. In a 1944 case, the judge commented:

> it can hardly ever be applicable where the act to which the servant is said to be 'volens' arises out of his ordinary duty, *unless the work for which he is engaged is one in which danger is necessarily involved* (Bowater v Rowley Regis Corp.).[26]

In the context of workplace stress claims it is difficult to envisage many situations in which a successful defence could be made out, although recent judicial comment has hinted at its applicability. For example, in the case of the Hillsborough police officers *(Frost and Others v Chief Constable of S. Yorks and Others;* see note 23), the judge's attitude was that:

> it is part of a police officer's duty to deal with situations which might cause psychiatric harm to ordinary people.

In a similar vein, the judge who would have held Chris Johnstone bound by the express terms of his contract (see pages 44–6) commented that:

> Before he accepted that obligation he knew what it would entail . . . Those who cannot stand the heat should stay out of the kitchen.

Such a view did not, however, find favour with one of the judge's colleagues, who thought the principle, if applied to aspiring doctors, would have serious implications, because the NHS was effectively a monopoly employer that demanded one year's practice as a house officer in a hospital.

All that can fairly be said in conclusion is that the defence of volenti remains a possibility to be raised in an appropriate case – perhaps, for instance, where an inherently stressful job is highly paid and the court were to regard the level of remuneration as a form of 'danger money' (see the case of *Withers* v *Perry Chain Co Ltd*,[27] also discussed on page 127).

Contributory negligence

In a case in which negligence is proved, the defendant may submit that the plaintiff was guilty of contributory negligence in that, by failing to act reasonably, he or she was partly to blame for the injury.

A successful submission of contributory negligence does not get the defendant off the hook entirely: it is merely a partial defence, the effect of which is to reduce plaintiffs' damages by the extent to which they negligently contribute to their injury. Contributory negligence may also be proved where a plaintiff's lack of care does not contribute to the 'accident' itself but merely to the extent of the injury suffered – for example, the failure by a person involved in a road traffic accident to wear a seat belt.

In the context of psychiatric harm in the workplace, employees might be found to have failed to take reasonable care of themselves and, in so doing, contributed to their injury if, for example:

☐ the employer was in breach of the duty of care by overloading the employee, but the employee had failed properly to delegate work to others

☐ the employer was vicariously liable for harassment by a colleague or superior of the employee, but the employee had neglected to make use of a grievance procedure found to be suitable for complaints of harassment

☐ the employer was negligent in failing to provide sufficient security in a retail outlet, but the employee unreasonably refused the counselling made available following (say) a raid.

Summary

To succeed in a personal injury case based on workplace stress the employee must prove that, on the balance of probabilities (ie that it is more probable than not):

☐ the employer could reasonably have foreseen the risk of psychiatric harm to that group of employees of which the plaintiff is a member, or to him or her specifically

☐ the employer failed to take such steps as were reasonable in the circumstances to protect the employee from the risk of harm

☐ the employee suffered psychiatric harm that was caused by the employer's failure to take those steps.

References

1 [1937] 3 All ER 628, H.L.

2 [1995] IRLR 35.

3 A tort is a civil wrong, as opposed to a criminal wrong (crime).

4 *Rorrison* v *West Lothian College and Lothian Regional Council*, IDS Brief 655 p5, Court of Session, 21.7.99.

5 BIFU. *The Hidden Cost – Survey of bank and building society robberies*. London, BIFU Publications, 1992.

6 Richards D. A. and Deale A. 'The effect of a raid on society staff.' Unpublished report for Nationwide Building Society, 1990.

7 ICD – 10 para F43.1, p344.

8 American Psychiatric Association. *Diagnostic and Statistical Manual of Mental Disorders*. 4th edn. International Version, Washington DC, American Psychiatric Association, 1995. (DSM-IV) para 309.81. Note: DSM-IV International Version adopts the ICD-10 coding (ie para F43.1.)

9 [1993] ICR 789.

10 [1991] IRLR 118.

11 [1984] 1 All ER 997.

12 See *Law Commission Report on Liability for Psychiatric Illness*. Law Com. No. 249, HMSO, 1998.

13 [1991] 4 All ER 907.
14 [1998] 3 WLR 1509, [1998] 1 AER 1.
15 [1967] 1 WLR 912.
16 [1951] 1 LR 271.
17 [1995] IRLR 251.
18 This argument was also rejected in the case of White – see note 14.
19 [1983] 133 NLJ 870.
20 *The Times*, 4 February 1986.
21 18 January 1995, referred to in *Robertson and Rough* v *Forth Road Bridge Joint Board*, note 17.
22 [1993] PIQR Q30.
23 9 April 1995.
24 [1952] 1 All ER 1302.
25 [1991] 104 ACTR 1.
26 [1944] 1 All ER 465.
27 [1961] 3 All ER 676.

5 STATUTORY PROVISIONS RELEVANT TO WORKPLACE STRESS

Introduction

In Chapter 4 the legal issues involved in common law personal injury actions were explored. In effect they are simply an extension of employers' existing duty to their employees in respect of health and safety to risks to mental well-being.

In contrast, this chapter brings together various pieces of existing legislation that employers should now look at afresh, because they can all, in one way or another, impose liability for workplace stress. Some of them are principally criminal statutes, by virtue of which the employer can face fines or prosecution; others are statutory provisions that allow employees a right of access to employment tribunals and awards of compensation for successful applications.

Health and safety legislation

The Health and Safety at Work Act (HASAWA) 1974

Most responsible employers are aware of their obligations under this legislation, so far as they relate to guarding against physical injury. The Act was novel in its time because it covered all workplaces and everyone at work, and also because, in contrast to the common law, which merely compensated employees who had already suffered an injury, it was intended to have a preventive effect. Its central aim was to 'secure the health, safety and welfare of persons at work', and this was to be effected by placing duties on both employers and employees. Breach of the duties would lead to criminal liability. Now that it has been established by the Walker case (see Chapter 4) that mental health is no different in principle from physical health in the context of the duty of care, employers will need to be aware of risks to mental health when carrying out their duties under the Act. The message has been reinforced by the publication of guidelines on stress at work by the HSE[1] (which polices the Act). These guidelines state that:

> employers . . . have a legal duty to take reasonable care to ensure that health is not placed at risk through excessive and sustained levels of stress arising from the way work is organised, the way people deal with each other at their work or from the day-to-day demands placed on their workplace.

> . . . stress should be treated like any other health hazard.

Detailed discussion of the provisions of HASAWA is outside the scope of this book, but the following points should be noted:

☐ The overall duty on employers under section 2(1) is 'to ensure, so far as is reasonably practicable, the health, safety and welfare at work of all employees'.

☐ As in the case of the common-law duty of care (see Chapter 4), the statute does not require employers to avoid risks to health at all costs. What is reasonably practicable is a cost/benefit exercise, and 'practicable' is not to be equated with 'physically possible'. In *West Bromwich Building Society Ltd v Townsend*,[2] the society had been served with an improvement notice requiring them to install bandit screens, and this was upheld by an employment tribunal. An appeal to the High Court was allowed on the basis that the tribunal had considered only whether it was physically and financially possible to fit the screens, rather than weighing the risk against the cost.

☐ If it is shown that the employer has not complied with a duty under the Act, section 40 provides that the burden is on the employer to satisfy the court (on the balance of probabilities) that it was not reasonably practicable to do so in the circumstances, in order to escape liability.

In addition to the general duty in section 2(1), there are also specific duties in respect of which workplace stress should be borne in mind, eg:

☐ to provide and maintain safe plant and systems of work (section 2(2)(a)). This could be relevant not only where employees suffer stress because they have to use unsafe machinery or equipment, but also as a result of, for example, oppressive shift systems, management methods or job content.

☐ to make arrangements for ensuring safety and absence of risks to health in connection with the use, handling, storage and transport of articles and substances (section 2(2)(b)). The HSE guidelines specifically point to the stressful effects of working in 'the presence of toxic or dangerous materials or other obvious workplace hazards which might not be adequately controlled'.

☐ to provide information, instruction, training and supervision so as to ensure employees' health and safety (section 2(2)(c)). This implies that employers must first familiarise themselves with sources of stress at work and the steps that can be taken to alleviate it.

☐ to provide and maintain a working environment that is safe, without risks to health, and adequate as regards facilities and arrangements for employees' welfare (section 2(2)(e)). Stressful aspects of the working environment are likely to include noise, heat, vibration and humidity.

☐ where there are more than five employees, to draw up a written policy statement on health and safety at work, and bring it to employees' attention (section 2(3)). Presumably, employers should now include specific references to psychological health in their company health and safety documentation.

☐ to consult with safety representatives (appointed by recognised trade unions) and allow them to check the adequacy of safety measures (section 2(6)).

☐ to establish safety committees if requested to do so by safety representatives (section 2(7)).

The Act is enforced by the HSE through its inspectorate, which has the power to prosecute for breaches of the Act. However, a characteristic of the inspectorate in the UK has been the emphasis placed on informal action by way of giving advice, and so far the HSE has limited itself to attempting to raise awareness among organisations to their responsibility for mental health as well as physical well-being. More recently, concern over the lack of action taken in response to its exhortations has led the HSE to consider drawing up an Approved Code of Practice on workplace stress.

Employers who wish to become well informed in advance of any intervention by the HSE will find not only the HSE guidelines useful but also the earlier research report that led to the guidelines.[3] Although non-compliance with HSE guidelines (and any Health and Safety Commission Approved Code of Practice) does not constitute an offence in itself, such non-compliance may be relevant as evidence of contravention of a statutory requirement (see S17 HASAWA). The standard introduction to HSE guidance states that:

> Following the guidance is not compulsory and you are free to take other action. But if you do follow the guidance you will normally be doing enough to comply with the law.

The Management of Health and Safety at Work (MHSW) Regulations 1992

Employers who take seriously their obligations under HASAWA are likely to have already carried out risk assessments in their workplaces. However, it was only with the passing of these Regulations that employers first came under a statutory duty to do so, in order that hazards to health could be identified and appropriate preventive or protective measures taken to remove or at least reduce them. The case of *Thompson, Gray and Nicholson* v *Smiths Shiprepairers (North Shields) Ltd*[4] was a common-law claim for damages, but its ruling has particular relevance for the new obligation on employers to include risks to mental health in their assessments. The High Court held that:

> While there is a type of risk which is regarded at any given time as an inescapable feature of industry and the employer is not liable for the consequences of that risk, changes in social awareness, or improvements in knowledge and technology may subsequently transfer the risk into the category of those against which the employer can and should take care. In this context, a breach of duty consists not only of failing to take precautions known to

be available as a means of combating a known danger but also of not taking the initiative in seeking out knowledge of facts which are not themselves obvious.

Since the date of the *Walker* judgment (November 1994) the risk to employees' mental health is one that has been laid at the feet of employers to be included in their duty of care. The Regulations themselves do not define the term 'risk', but the accompanying Code of Practice states that:

(a) a hazard is something with the potential to cause harm (this can include substances or machines, methods of work and other aspects of work organisation);

(b) risk expresses the likelihood that the harm from a particular hazard is realised;

(c) the extent of risk; ie the number of people who might be exposed and the consequences for them.

Risk therefore reflects both the likelihood that harm will occur and its severity (Paragraph 5).

The MHSW Regulations potentially require employers to:

☐ make themselves aware, through current literature, of the sources of stress at work, and how these may be affecting their own organisation

☐ assess risks to the mental health of their workforce (and of others who may be affected by the organisation's activities)

☐ make arrangements for putting into practice the necessary preventive and protective measures

☐ carry out, where appropriate, a health surveillance

☐ give adequate information and training about risks.

Since the Regulations were amended in 1994, employers have been under a duty specifically to assess the risks to women who are of childbearing age and who may be pregnant, have recently (ie within the previous six months) given birth or be breastfeeding (Regulations 13A). If the risks exposed cannot be avoided by preventive action, a woman who has notified her employer that she is pregnant must be suspended from work for as long as it is necessary to protect her health and safety. However, sections 67 and 68 of the Employment Rights Act 1996 now also provide that, before being suspended, such a woman has the right to be offered any suitable alternative work, and that during suspension she has the right to be paid.

Breach of the MHSW Regulations normally attracts criminal liability but, exceptionally, where an employer fails to carry out the duty under Regulation 13A and the woman or her baby suffers damage, the latter are given the right to a civil claim for damages for breach of statutory duty. (The child could also sue under the Congenital Disabilities Act 1976.) Employers would do well to take this issue seriously: in one case a woman police sergeant who alleged that working in a domestic violence unit caused her to have a miscarriage was awarded £15,000 in an out-of-court settlement. She had complained formally on two occasions about the stress of dealing with battered wives and, following the loss of her baby, initiated a sex discrimination claim.[5]

The Health and Safety (Display Screen Equipment) Regulations 1992

Because work with display screen equipment can lead to certain muscular problems, eye fatigue and mental stress, employers need to familiarise themselves with the duties laid down in these Regulations. They cover such matters as providing information and training, planning work to allow for breaks, assessing workstations, reducing risks discovered and making sure that workstations satisfy minimum requirements for the display screen itself. (Note also the requirement for risk assessment under the Control of Substances Hazardous to Health Regulations 1988.)

Employment protection legislation

Dismissal for capability (including ill-health)

The Employment Rights Act (ERA) 1996 protects employees by giving them the right not to be unfairly dismissed (section 94) and providing employers with only a limited number of potentially fair reasons for dismissal. One such reason (under section 98(2)(a)) relates 'to the capability or qualifications of the employee for performing work of the kind which he was employed to do', and it is specifically stated in section 98(3) that 'capability' is assessed with respect to 'health or any other physical or mental quality'.

As a consequence of these provisions, it is potentially fair to dismiss not only incompetent employees but also those whose health prevents them from doing their job, and presumably those whose mental constitution means that they cannot cope with the demands of the job. The section can also cover employees who suffer a stress-related illness caused by some aspect of the working environment, as the case of *London Fire and Civil Defence Authority* v *Betty*[6] made clear. In that case Mr Betty suffered a nervous breakdown as a result of accusations by his employer of racial discrimination and harassment of his fellow employees. He never fully recovered from the nervous breakdown and was eventually retired on medical grounds. The Employment Appeal Tribunal (EAT) warned tribunals not to be concerned about whether the illness that brought about the dismissal was caused by the employer. The EAT stated that employers who injured their employees were not thereby prevented from dismissing them fairly – although, unsurprisingly, the EAT also pointed out that if the injury was caused by a breach of duty on the part of the employer, the employee would be entitled to the appropriate compensation (ie in a civil action; see Chapter 4).

However, an employee may be unfairly dismissed, and hence entitled to compensation, even if the employer believes that he or she is not capable of doing the job. This is because the 1996 Act makes it clear, first, that it is for the employer to show what the reason was for the dismissal (section 98(1)(a)) and, second, that:

> whether the dismissal was fair...shall depend on whether in the circumstances (including the size and administrative resources of the employer's undertaking) the employer acted reasonably or unreasonably in treating it as a sufficient reason for dismissing the employee; and that question shall be determined in accordance with equity and the substantial merits of the case (section 98(4)).

It is thus fundamental to a fair dismissal related to capability that the employer has established clearly the medical position and followed a fair procedure. In theory, an employer may wish to dismiss employees who cannot cope with the job even if they have taken no time off work, but because absenteeism is an invariable response to stress and inability to cope, it will be assumed that the particular employee will have shown some pattern of absences. The Act does not distinguish between persistent absenteeism and long-term absences, but examination of case law reveals that some differences in approach may be necessary, depending on whether employers are dealing with repeated absences due to transient complaints or a situation in which there is an underlying medical condition.

Persistent absenteeism

In this situation, the cases of *International Sport Co* v *Thomson*[7] and *Lynock* v *Cereal Packaging Ltd*[8] are particularly relevant. Employers wishing to dismiss employees who are persistently absent, even for short periods, should follow a fair procedure consisting of these steps:

1 Identify the persistent absentee. This implies the existence of an absence control policy, which in large organisations may be fairly sophisticated. However, whatever mechanism is used, employers need to ensure that they obtain accurate information about absences and monitor them sufficiently to see whether a coherent pattern emerges. Where an employee has an unacceptable level of intermittent absences due to minor ailments, what is required is, first, that there should be a fair review by the employer of the attendance record (*Thomson* case). Obtaining accurate information also helps to ensure consistency of treatment between employees.

2 Carry out an investigation to find out the reason for the absences. This will generally involve interviewing the employee and listening to any explanation that the employee puts forward. There is not always a duty to take detailed medical advice, because:

> where one is dealing with intermittent periods of illness, each of which is unconnected, it seems to us to be impossible to give a reasonable prognosis or projection of the possibility of what will happen in the future.
>
> (*Lynock* case)

Nevertheless, in the context of absences for stress-related

illnesses it may be important to make sufficient enquiries to determine whether or not there is some underlying medical condition brought about by the working environment.

3 Explain to the employee that the attendance pattern is unacceptable, that an improvement is necessary, and what the consequences will be of a failure to improve. It has been stated that:

> these cases are not cases of disciplinary situations; what is important is that employers should treat each case individually where there is a genuine illness and with sympathy, understanding and compassion. The jargon of the Industrial Relations [Code is] in terms of warnings, but really that is not the purpose of the system operated by an employer; it is to give a caution that the stage has been reached where with the best will in the world it becomes impossible to continue with the employment.
>
> (*Lynock* case)

Of course, if an illness is found not to be genuine, then employers are entitled to treat the related absences as disciplinary offences. Nevertheless, it is generally felt that to establish whether each and every absence is genuine or not may be unhelpful. Employers often take the view that it is preferable to treat the absences as genuine but unacceptable once they reach a certain level.

4 Make a decision to dismiss having taken account of such factors as:

- □ the nature of the illness
- □ the likelihood that it or some other illness may recur
- □ the length of the various absences
- □ the periods of good health between them
- □ the need of the employer to have the work done by the particular employee
- □ the impact of the absence on others who work with the employee
- □ the extent to which the difficulty of the situation and the position of the employer have been made clear to the employee (*Lynock* case).

Long-term ill-health or underlying medical condition

Here the emphasis is very much on investigating the medical condition and consulting with the employee (see the case of *East Lyndsay D.C.* v *Daubney*).[9] A fair procedure is thus likely to involve:

1 seeking medical advice. Relying on medical certificates is not normally sufficient: advice should come from a qualified medical practitioner. Because a knowledge of what the job involves is necessary, the company's own doctor may be the preferred choice, but employees should be allowed to put forward their own specialist's report in addition. The process often involves asking the employee to undergo a medical examination, and it may be fair to dismiss employees who refuse to co-operate with an employer who is seeking to ascertain the medical position. Nevertheless, as the case of *Cartwright* v *Post Office*[10] demonstrates, employers should not act too hastily. The applicant had been off work suffering from anxiety, depression and possibly a duodenal ulcer for some seven months when he was told that a medical examination had been arranged for him with the occupational health service. Although Mr Cartwright had no objection in principle to complying, he wanted to postpone the examination to a date when his own medical report would be available. The reason for this was that he had been given to understand that a significant purpose of the examination would be to enable consideration of his being medically retired, and in his view this was premature. When he refused to attend he was dismissed. The tribunal had no hesitation in finding that his dismissal was unfair, because no substantial reason for dismissal had been established, although it should be pointed out that the respondent made no real attempt to defend the claim and failed to attend the tribunal hearing.

Based on the medical advice, employers should consider these questions:

☐ What is the prognosis?
☐ How long is the employee likely to be absent from work?
☐ How long will it be before a replacement is necessary?

☐ If the employee is absent with a stress-related illness, is it likely to recur if the employee returns to work?

2 consulting with the employee. In *Taylorplan Catering (Scotland) Ltd* v *McInally*,[11] the EAT held that, apart from considerations of general courtesy, the reason for consultation was to:

> secure that the situation can be weighed up, balancing the employer's need for the work to be done, on the one hand, against the employee's time to recover his health on the other.

Consultation will be especially important where investigation of the employee's condition has shown that it may have been brought about by some aspect of the working environment. Although (as established in the London Fire and Civil Defence Authority case, see page 66) employers are not prevented from dismissing fairly in these circumstances, a tribunal is unlikely to find that an employer has acted reasonably in the circumstances if there were practicable remedial steps that could have been taken (see eg *Piggott Bros* v *Jackson*).[12]

3 considering the alternatives to dismissal. If consultation has shown that there are steps that could be taken to reduce the risk of a recurrence of the stress-related illness, the practicability of such steps should be considered. They may include:

☐ providing the employee with extra assistance (see the *Walker* case, Chapter 4)

☐ removing the source of the stress, eg dismissing or relocating an individual who has been found to have harassed or bullied the employee

☐ providing the employee with counselling, especially if the employee has domestic as well as workplace pressures

☐ altering some physical aspect of the work environment, eg noise levels

☐ considering an alternative, less stressful job.

These alternatives should be considered in consultation with the employee; if none is appropriate, or the job is inherently stressful, then it may be fair to dismiss. Merely because the employee's period of sick pay has not been exhausted does not mean that a decision to dismiss cannot be made (see *Cross* v *Cumberland Building Society*, pages 139–143); conversely, it may be unfair to dismiss employees as soon as their sick pay runs out. Two further points should be noted in this context: frustration of contract, and health and safety dismissals.

Frustration of contract

It has been held that the doctrine of frustration of contract can be applied to employment contracts. A contract is frustrated when some event occurs that is outside the control of the parties to the contract, and that makes further performance illegal, impossible or radically different from what was envisaged at the time the contract was made. Its applicability to instances of long-term ill-health is discussed in the cases of *Marshall* v *Harland and Woolf Ltd*[13] and *Egg Stores* v *Leibovici*.[14] In the latter case the EAT stated:

> There will have been frustration of the contract, even though at the time of the event (ie the employee's illness) the outcome was uncertain, if the time comes when, looking back, one can say that at some point matters had gone on so long, and the prospects for future employment were so poor, that it was no longer practical to regard the contract as still subsisting.

Relevant considerations were held to include:

- the employee's length of service
- how long the employment had been expected to continue
- the nature of the job
- the nature, length and effect of the disabling event
- the need for the work to be done by a replacement (rather than being covered by other workers)
- the risk of acquiring unfair dismissal or redundancy obligations to a replacement
- whether wages have continued to be paid
- whether, in all the circumstances, a reasonable employer could be expected to wait any longer before replacing the employee on a permanent basis.

The legal significance of a frustrating event is that the contract terminates automatically, and in the context of an employment contract there is therefore no dismissal and hence no possibility of an unfair dismissal claim. Possibly for this reason, and because its application consequently relieves employers of their obligations to manage an ill-health dismissal by means of a fair procedure, tribunals are reluctant to hold that an employee's ill-health is a frustrating event (see eg *Williams* v *Watson Luxury Coaches*).[15]

Health and safety dismissals

Although, in general, employees qualify for the right not to be unfairly dismissed only when they have one year's continuous service (section 108(1)), this is not so in the case of so-called 'health and safety dismissals' under section 100 of the ERA. For example, section 100(1)(c) provides that a dismissal is automatically unfair if the reason for it is that the employee 'brought to his employer's attention, by reasonable means, circumstances connected with his work which he reasonably believed were harmful or potentially harmful to health and safety'. In the case of *Cartwright* v *Post Office* discussed earlier (see page 69), the applicant was purportedly dismissed for failing to observe a reasonable management instruction. However, this was contested by the applicant, who stated:

> Whatever the respondents say I was dismissed because of health and safety reasons. I had long complained about my working environment. The environment was wrong because of positive management hostility and practice and behaviour.

Mr Cartwright's counsel submitted that this brought his dismissal within section 100 (1)(c), but his submission was rejected by the tribunal on the basis that:

> The applicant was not complaining about dangerous conditions such as poor ventilation or insufficient light or anything of that sort but was simply finding the working environment intolerable because of the pressures on him and more particularly the behaviour of his line manager. We do not believe that this is what section 100 is about.

With respect to the tribunal, this was an unnecessarily narrow interpretation of the section, and a much broader interpretation has recently been sanctioned by the EAT in the case of *Harvest Press Ltd* v *McCaffrey*.[16] Mr McCaffrey was assigned to the night shift with a considerably younger colleague, Mr Huson. On a particular evening when they were alone together, Mr Huson became so abusive to Mr McCaffrey that he decided to telephone his manager. While attempting to make the call, Mr Huson stood over Mr McCaffrey and shouted abuse at him, so alarming Mr McCaffrey that he decided to drive home and call his manager from there. When Mr McCaffrey subsequently refused to return to work unless he received assurances about his safety, he was regarded as having resigned and sent his P45.

The EAT had no hesitation in finding that Mr McCaffrey had in fact been dismissed and that the dismissal fell within section 100(1)(d) of the ERA because the reason for it was that 'in circumstances of danger which the employee reasonably believed to be serious and imminent and which he could not reasonably have been expected to avert, he left...his place of work'. They upheld the view of the tribunal that the word 'danger' was not limited to dangers arising out of the workplace but could include the circumstances of danger caused by the behaviour of other workers.

The important message of this case is that some forms of bullying may give rise to an action under section 100 – and since the passing of the Employment Relations Act 1999, there is no limit to the amount of compensation that can be awarded in such cases.

Constructive dismissal

Under section 95(1)(c) of the ERA, employees can claim to be dismissed, and hence able to bring a case of unfair dismissal, if they resign in response to conduct on the part of the employer that entitles them to terminate the contract. In common parlance, they are 'constructively' dismissed. The case of *Western Excavating Ltd* v *Sharp*[17] established that the conduct in question must amount to a fundamental breach of the contract of employment by the employer.

Sometimes employees bring such claims on the basis that the employer has breached an express term of their contract, for example by cutting pay or enforcing a change in contractual hours. However, of more relevance to workplace stress are those cases in which employees complain that there has been a breach of the implied term in the contract of employment that employers:

> will not, without reasonable and proper cause, conduct themselves in a manner calculated or likely to destroy or seriously damage the relationship of confidence and trust between the employer and the employee (*Woods* v *WM Car Services (Peterborough) Ltd*).[18]

Employees who bring such claims are basically saying that they have been treated so badly that they could not stand it any longer, and it is not unusual to find that they have suffered stress-related illnesses. Two examples illustrate this point.

In *Leech* v *CRS*[19] a check-out manageress was reluctantly persuaded to take on the additional role of cash-office supervisor in order to sort out the problem of cash shortages. Despite being reluctant she was given insufficient training and support to carry out her extra duties. On occasions when Mrs Leech did report instances of theft the police were not called in; her line manager's response to her notifying him of cash shortages was to instruct her to put in refunds to cover up the situation. A new computer was installed while Mrs Leech was on holiday, and although the system proved totally unsatisfactory, her line manager failed to respond to her requests for assistance and left it to her to call for extra help to sort the problem out. Mrs Leech went on sick leave and submitted a grievance, but no action was taken. The police were finally called in over another matter that, on her return to work, Mrs Leech had brought to her employer's attention. She was interviewed by the police and made to feel that the finger of suspicion pointed at her; she resigned when she herself was suspended, pending further investigation.

Mrs Leech suffered a depressive illness that left her unable to work for a period of nine months. The tribunal had no hesitation in finding that she had been (unfairly) constructively dismissed. It stated:

> it seems to us that this is a clear case where an honest, loyal and long-serving employee was utterly demoralised and frustrated by being deprived totally of the management support to which she was entitled, and ultimately felt she had become the object of the very suspicions she had been set up to police.

She was awarded compensation, including loss of wages for the nine-month period during which she was too ill to work.

In *Fry v Ashton Decor and Garden Centre*[20] a florist's assistant claimed that she had been forced out of her job by her employer's behaviour, and that the stress of working with him had caused her to suffer from Bell's Palsy. The tribunal found Ms Fry's employer to have been guilty of a number of breaches of contract which cumulatively entitled her to resign. In particular, the employer:

☐ caused her to work in conditions so cold that she suffered arthritis in her hands and feet (breach of implied duty to take reasonable care of employee's health and safety)

☐ required her to work longer hours than those contractually specified and 'paid' her for the extra hours only in kind (express breach)

☐ disciplined her in a threatening and abusive manner (breach of implied term that the employer will not destroy relationship of mutual trust and confidence – note relevance to bullying)

☐ unilaterally cancelled the occupational pension that he had agreed to set up for the applicant in lieu of her receiving an annual pay rise (express breach).

Although constructive dismissal cases may be brought where the fundamental breach arises out of a single act by the employer, it is much more common, particularly where the employee resigns suffering from symptoms of stress, for there to have been (as in the cases of *Leech* and *Fry* above) a build-up over a period of time. Following a 'last straw' incident the employee finally decides to go.

The implications for employers anxious not to find themselves with such cases on their hands are that, where possible, they should avoid:

☐ forcing promotions on employees who are not capable of doing a more demanding job

☐ leaving employees without proper management support

☐ making unilateral changes to employees' contracts of employment

☐ disciplining employees in a threatening or abusive manner

□ victimising or harassing employees (see the discussion of discrimination legislation below)

□ subjecting employees to a stressful working environment, eg one that is unsafe or subject to extremes of temperature.

Even though the test for constructive dismissal is a contractual one, the question of whether employers have behaved reasonably is likely to be a relevant factor in deciding whether they have destroyed the relationship of mutual trust and confidence. Employees will not be found to have been constructively dismissed simply because they resign suffering from stress.

For example, in the case of *Hobbs* v *British Railways Board*[21] a work colleague was accused of indecently assaulting Mr Hobbs's stepdaughter. This incident caused Mr Hobbs and his family considerable stress and anxiety. Although the two men did not work at the same depot, they did come into contact from time to time, which Mr Hobbs found very distressing; this situation resulted in his taking sick leave. Following investigations into the incident, management took steps to minimise the contact between Mr Hobbs and his colleague, but Mr Hobbs wanted to be transferred to a different depot. Although his employers did not reject this out of hand, they felt it more appropriate to postpone any decision until after the impending criminal trial. It was similarly decided that no decision to dismiss the accused man should be made until this time. By now Mr Hobbs was on sick leave again, and although his employers made it clear that his job was not in jeopardy, he resigned some four weeks later.

The tribunal held that British Railways Board had not failed to provide Mr Hobbs with the necessary support, and it was not unreasonable of them to have postponed the request for a transfer and the decision about the accused man's future with the company until after the trial. They had not therefore breached the implied term of trust and confidence.

Discrimination legislation

The Sex Discrimination Act (SDA) 1975 and the Race Relations Act (RRA) 1976

These Acts are couched in similar terms, proscribing unlawful discrimination and giving victims of discrimination the right of access to employment tribunals. Section 1(1)(a) of the SDA defines discrimination as less favourable treatment on grounds of sex,[22] whereas section 1(1)(a) of the RRA refers to less favourable treatment on racial grounds.[23] Employment lawyers invariably refer to this as 'direct' discrimination: it involves a comparison of how a person of one sex (or racial group) is treated compared with the way in which a person not of that sex (or racial group) is, or would be, treated. In other words, a hypothetical comparison is permitted.

However, a finding that a particular woman has been treated less favourably than a particular man does not of itself constitute discrimination, because in order to discriminate within the SDA, the less favourable treatment must be on grounds of sex. For example, a woman sacked because she is unreliable is not discriminated against when a man fulfilling his job requirements is kept on: the treatment is not 'on grounds of sex'. In deciding whether there is discrimination, the House of Lords have held that the question to be considered is 'Would the complainant have received the same treatment...but for his or her sex?' (see *James* v *Eastleigh B. C.*).[24]

The Acts also cover treatment that is fair in form but discriminatory in its impact. Such treatment is defined in section 1(1)(b) of each Act and is commonly known as 'indirect' discrimination. Examples are unjustified application of such things as height requirements or lifting requirements, or unjustifiably specifying a degree from a UK university for a job. Although this is an important feature of recruitment practices in particular, it is less relevant for the purposes of this book, and hence attention will be focused on direct discrimination.

Section 6 of the SDA and section 4 of the RRA set out what kinds of discrimination are unlawful. They include discrimination by failing to offer a person employment; in the way in which access is afforded to promotion or other benefits; and by dismissing a person or subjecting him or her to a detriment. Sexual and racial harassment are now generally accepted as being unlawful discrimination because they are forms of less favourable treatment on grounds of sex or race that subject individuals to a detriment in terms of their working environment.

The reason this legislation is relevant in considering liability for workplace stress is that individuals who are subjected to unlawful discrimination generally find the experience hurtful, distressing and humiliating; Parliament has recognised this by providing specifically for compensation for injury to feelings in addition to any award for lost earnings and the like (section 66(4) SDA, section 57(4) RRA). In 1992 the EAT stated that injury to feelings was almost inevitable in sex discrimination cases (*Murray* v *Powertech (Scotland) Ltd*)[25] and that £500 was at, or near, the minimum compensation (*Sharifi* v *Strathclyde Regional Council*).[26]

The type of unlawful discrimination most likely to cause stress and stress-related illnesses is sexual or racial harassment or abuse. A study of 21 applicants to employment tribunals who alleged sexual harassment at work found that all had suffered negative physical and psychosocial outcomes, ranging from sickness, anger, anxiety, tiredness, fear, sleep problems, weight loss, relationship problems, depression and loss of confidence to nervous breakdown. Half the group had had to seek medical help and were prescribed such drugs as sleeping pills and antidepressants.[27]

Employers may be found liable for sexual or racial harassment in one of two ways. First, the legislation provides (in section 32(1) of the RRA and section 41(1) of the SDA) that 'anything done by a person in the course of his employment shall be treated...as done by his employer as well as by him'. Thus, as in the case of personal injury actions (see Chapter 4), employers are vicariously liable for the unlawful acts of their employees. However, there is an important difference: in the case of *Tower Boot Co Ltd* v *Jones*[28] the Court of Appeal took the view that, in statutory discrimination claims, the phrase 'in the course of employment' should be given its 'ordinary, everyday meaning' rather than applying the common law test of whether the behaviour in question could be regarded as an 'unauthorised mode of doing an authorised act'. Although this is likely to mean that employers will be liable for any harassment occurring at work (or even at a works-related social function, as was the case in *Stubbs* v *(1) Chief Constable of Lincolnshire Police and (2) Walker*),[29] it should be remembered that employers do have available a statutory defence in such cases. However, the defence applies only where the employer has done all that was reasonably practicable to *prevent* the doing of the unlawful act. Unless it can be shown that, for example, relevant staff training and/or effective policies were in place, a tribunal is likely to take the view that, even though prompt remedial action may have been taken, the necessary preventive measures were not.

Employers may also discriminate directly where, for example, they are aware that harassment is occurring and do nothing to prevent it, or where they fail to take seriously a complaint of harassment. In the case of *Burton & Rhule* v *De Vere Hotels Ltd*,[30] it was held that employers subject their employees to the detriment of sexual or racial harassment if they are in a position to control whether it happens or not (even where the harasser is not one of their own employees – in this case, the controversial comedian Bernard Manning).

Since around 1989 awards for injury to feelings in harassment cases, and indeed discrimination cases generally, have risen dramatically. Three developments in particular are likely to have been influential in bringing about the increase. First, there has been a welcome change in attitude to harassment cases, with a growing awareness of the seriousness of its consequences and a decreased likelihood of harassment being seen as something of a joke. Secondly, tribunals are, or should be, aware of a decision of the Court of Appeal in 1988 (*Alexander* v *The Home Office*)[31] in which the Court stated that damages for injury to feelings should reflect compensation for the consequences of the discrimination and that it 'should not be minimal because this would tend to trivialise or diminish respect for the public policy to which the Act gives effect'. Finally, there was the remarkable victory by Miss Marshall who (in the case of *Marshall (No 2)* v *Southampton & S.W. Hants Area Health Authority*)[32] successfully challenged the compensation limit of £11,000 under the SDA (at the time of the judgment), leading to a change in the law. The Sex Discrimination and Equal Pay (Remedies) Regulations 1993 (and shortly afterwards the Race Relations (Remedies) Act 1994) removed completely the ceiling on awards of compensation, resulting in their increasing by 45 per cent between January 1993 and June 1994. By this later date awards for injury to feelings were averaging £1,846,[33] and by 1998 the figure had reached £3,058.[34]

Aggravated damages may also be awarded where the employer behaved in a high-handed, malicious, insulting or oppressive manner in committing the act of discrimination, as happened in the case of *Ruizo* v *(1) Tesco Stores Ltd and (2) Lea*.[35] The applicant was an American of Spanish/Filipino origin who had been discriminated against on grounds of race. His compensation for injury to feelings was increased from £2,500 to £4,100 because of the employer's lack of contrition and continuing failure to address the problem of racial abuse. The company did not appear to see that the name-calling carried on by both management and the applicant's work colleagues was wrong: right up until the first tribunal hearing the company maintained that this was part of normal workplace banter.

The following examples illustrate tribunal awards in which employees have received substantial sums for injury to feelings.

1 *Hextall* v *The Post Office*[36]

A postal worker endured a campaign of harassment from her line manager over a period of 12 months. She took out a grievance against him but, despite the finding that much of what she complained about was true, he was not disciplined. As a result, she was off work for eight months with stress.

Injury to feelings: £15,000, including £5,000 aggravated damages.

2 *McLaughlin* v *London Borough of Southwark*[37]

An assistant director in Southwark's social services department who found her work being reallocated to male officers was moved to less important posts in different departments and eventually made redundant following deletion of her original post. None of the male assistant directors were treated in this way. The proceedings had 'dragged on for nearly three years' and there was an 'inexcusable failure to provide information sought', thereby adding to the feeling of hurt.

Injury to feelings: £12,500, including aggravated damages.

3 *A* v *B*[38]

A 21-year-old woman was sexually harassed over a period of three years by the owner of the software company for which she worked. The tribunal found that 'He persisted in his conduct [which] ... extended to physical touching, imposing an unreasonable timekeeping regime during which he might take advantage of her. The injury extended beyond the more usual humiliation and embarrassment to severe emotional and physical distress.'

Injury to feelings: £23,000.

4 *Mustafa* v (1) *Ancon Clark Ltd and (2) McNally*[39]
An Asian machine-setter was upset by racial remarks made by his supervisor. Despite his complaint, no effective action was taken by management. The following month he was subjected to a barrage of racial abuse from his supervisor and others and was subsequently off work with severe depression. By the date of his remedies hearing he had been off sick for two-and-a-half years, and his family life had been severely disrupted.
Injury to feelings: £20,000.

5 *Yeboah* v *(1) Crofton and (2) London Borough of Hackney*[40]
A Ghanaian-born head of personnel at Hackney Council was the target of a long series of false allegations from a director of housing of corruption, covering up corruption and improper behaviour. The tribunal found that the director had 'a fixed mental impression that Africans, particularly West Africans, had a propensity to commit fraud' and that his behaviour 'was grossly offensive and caused Mr Yeboah great distress. It interfered with his home life, caused him serious public humiliation and damaged his reputation.'
Injury to feelings: £45,000, including £10,000 aggravated damages. The award was made against the director of housing. (In addition, the local authority agreed to pay £380,000, including £40,000 for injury to feelings.)

As the above cases demonstrate, in many discrimination cases in which awards for injury to feelings are made the employee concerned has actually suffered a stress-related illness in addition to the emotions of distress and humiliation. The Court of Appeal has now made it plain that in successful discrimination claims, an employment tribunal is entitled to compensate applicants for any 'personal injury' *in addition* to awarding them compensation for injury to feelings.[41] This ruling is important, because if certain claims for personal injury can be brought in employment tribunals rather than via the civil courts, this will be a potentially much less expensive and procedurally simpler route for employees to take. Of greater significance legally, the Court of Appeal stated in their judgment that, in contrast to a claim in negligence (see Chapter 4), in which there is a requirement to establish reasonable foreseeability, 'this requirement does not need to be established' in a statutory discrimination claim.

The Court of Appeal's ruling has since been applied in the case of *Stubbs* v *(1) Chief Constable of Lincolnshire Police and (2) Walker* (see page 78), in which a detective constable suffered a depressive illness following sexual harassment over a 14-month period. The tribunal assessed Ms Stubbs's injury to health as moderately severe and awarded her £15,000, plus £25,000 injury to feelings (in addition to £1,506 against the harasser, Mr Walker).

Employers should note the following points:

☐ Employees who suffer a stress-related illness are also likely to be awarded compensation in respect of loss of earnings if they are unable to work.

☐ Employees with one year's service who are subjected to harassment or victimisation (or both) causing them to resign may claim constructive dismissal whether or not the harassment was based on sexual or racial grounds. (See eg *Wigan Borough Council* v *Davies*,[42] in which the council failed to take reasonable steps to see that Miss Davies was able to perform her duties without disruption and harassment from other members of staff.) Such cases could be brought either on the basis of a breach of the duty of reasonable care for the employee's health and safety or on the basis that the employer has destroyed the relationship of mutual trust and confidence. In other words, whereas the SDA and the RRA do not cover bullying if the employer is equally unpleasant to both sexes or to different racial groups (provided there are no sexual or racial overtones to the behaviour), the ERA does cover such bullying.

☐ In Northern Ireland employees are similarly protected against religious discrimination by the Fair Employment (Northern Ireland) Act 1976. (See eg *Duffy* v *Eastern Health and Social Services Board*,[43] which concerned a Catholic woman whose failure to obtain a permanent post as a laundry worker was held to constitute an act of unlawful discrimination, and who was awarded £15,000 injury to feelings, plus a further £5,000 aggravated damages.)

☐ They will be vicariously liable for unlawful acts of discrimination by their employees. However, they can ultimately escape liability if they can show that they took such steps as were reasonably practicable to prevent the doing of those acts (section 41(3) SDA, section 32(3) RRA).

☐ As is apparent from some of the case examples given above, tribunals can apportion any compensation between the employer and the individual discriminator. This is because the latter is regarded as 'aiding' the unlawful act of the employer (under section 42(1) of the SDA and section 33(1) of the RRA).

Disability Discrimination Act 1995 (DDA) 1995

This has been supplemented by the Disability Discrimination (Meaning of Disability) Regulations 1996, the Disability Discrimination (Employment) Regulations 1996, a Code of Practice and Guidance on matters to be taken into account in determining questions relating to the definition of disability.

After many years of upholding the voluntary approach to the employment of disabled persons, the UK Government finally conceded that neither this nor the quota scheme was working effectively. The DDA is the fruit of Parliament's efforts to find a legislative route to meeting such people's needs.[44]

The DDA defines discrimination using a format that is similar, but not identical, to that of 'direct' discrimination under the SDA and RRA. Whereas those Acts are couched in terms of less favourable treatment 'on grounds of' sex or race, the new Act provides that discrimination occurs when a disabled person is treated less favourably 'for a reason which relates to the person's disability'. Of more significance, perhaps, is the fact that, unlike under any previous legislation, here employers are allowed to discriminate if they are justified in doing so. In addition, although there are no provisions relating specifically to indirect discrimination, protection against practices that put disabled persons at a disadvantage is provided for by the employer's duty to make 'reasonable adjustment' within S6 of the Act. The duty arises where any arrangements made by or on behalf of an employer, or any physical feature of premises, place the disabled person concerned at a substantial disadvantage in comparison with persons who are not disabled.

It must be said that this legislation is extremely complex; anyone who has to get to grips with it, whether personnel practitioners or employment tribunal chairmen and lay members, will have their work cut out. More to the point, however, is the question whether the legislation is relevant for the purposes of this book.

Question 1: Does the Act cover stress-related illnesses?

The answer is that it may do but in any given case that can be determined only by close scrutiny of the definition of disability as set out in section 1(1) and supplemented by the provisions of Schedule 1. Thus, section 1(1) provides that a person has a 'disability' if:

> he has a physical or mental impairment which has a substantial and long-term adverse effect on his ability to carry out normal day-to-day activities.

A mental impairment is defined as including impairment from, or consisting of, a mental illness only if it is a clinically well-recognised illness. In the case of *Goodwin* v *Patent Office*,[45] the EAT advised tribunals to see whether the illness was mentioned in the *World Health Organisation's International Classification of Diseases* (see page 39). As in the case of personal injury actions, therefore, a person who claims to be suffering merely from 'stress' will not be regarded as disabled. In any case, to be 'long-term' an impairment must have lasted at least 12 months or must reasonably be expected to last for that long. Although, as the case studies in Chapter 6 make clear, many stress-related disorders are extremely long-lasting, others could be excluded by this provision. Mr Walker, for example, was off work for only four months when he had his first nervous breakdown (see Chapter 4). However, his condition could be brought within the ambit of the DDA by a further provision that an impairment that ceases to have a substantial and adverse[46] effect will be treated as continuing to have that effect if such effect is likely to recur.

The final determinant of whether a condition is treated as a disability is that its adverse effect must affect 'normal day-to-day activities'. These are exhaustively (and somewhat restrictively) set out in the Act to include only:

□ mobility
□ manual dexterity

- physical co-ordination
- continence
- ability to lift, carry, or otherwise move everyday objects
- speech, hearing, or eyesight
- memory or ability to concentrate, learn, or understand
- perception of the risk of physical danger.

But for the penultimate item in this list it might be unlikely that any stress-related illness would be treated as a disability, although the Guidance notes in Para C7 that 'where a person has a mental illness such as depression account should be taken of whether, although that person has the physical ability to perform a task, he or she is, in practice, unable to sustain an activity over a reasonable period'. It is also important to remember that in considering whether an impairment has a substantial and adverse effect on normal day-to-day activities, a tribunal is to consider what the situation would be if any treatment the employee is receiving were to be removed. Thus, in the case of *Kapadia* v *London Borough of Lambeth*,[47] the EAT held that the tribunal should have taken into account the effects that the employee's depression would have had were it not for the treatment he was receiving by way of counselling.

Question 2: How is the Act most likely to affect employers if it does cover stress-related illnesses?

If stress-related illnesses do count as a 'disability' for the purposes of the DDA, the two further questions that employers may ask themselves are, first, 'What happens if I exclude applicants with a history of mental disorder?' and, secondly, 'If employees who develop stress-related illnesses take sickness absence, does the Act prevent me from dismissing them?'

Screening out vulnerable applicants

It should be noted that the Bill in its original form did not cover individuals with a history of mental illness. However, during its passage through the House of Lords it was modified, as Lord Mackay explained:

It has become clear that people who have had a disability although they may no longer be disabled as such, share with people who are currently disabled a need for protection against discrimination in relation to their disability...In addition we have been persuaded that it is not always possible to tell when a person has fully recovered from a disability and when the condition is no longer likely to recur.[48]

An employer who refuses to employ a person purely and simply on the basis that, for example, he or she has had a nervous breakdown in the past is treating that person less favourably for a reason that relates to the disability. Such treatment amounts to 'direct' discrimination under the Act. However, as indicated earlier, the employer is allowed to justify discriminatory treatment, but only if the reason for the less favourable treatment is both 'material' to the circumstances of the particular case and 'substantial'. No clarification of the terms 'material' and 'substantial' is provided in the Act itself, although the government envisaged that, in a given case, account would have to be taken of such factors as the type of job and the type of disability, and its effects. The Code of Practice which accompanies the Act states that the reason has to relate to the individual circumstances in question and not just be 'trivial or minor', but even so employers may feel somewhat in the dark about this matter. It is conceivable, though, that they would be able to justify a decision not to appoint to an inherently stressful job a person with a past history of stress-related illness.

Dismissing employees suffering stress-related illnesses

The consequences of dismissing absent employees without going through fair procedures and taking reasonable steps to consult them have already been discussed in relation to liability for unfair dismissal. It is also clear that 'reasonable' employers will consider offering lighter work, should it be available, before taking a decision to dismiss. The duty to make 'reasonable adjustments' under section 6 of the DDA serves to reinforce those obligations by specifically listing examples (in section 6(3)) of the kinds of step employers may have to take in relation to a disabled person. In the context of stress-related illness they include:

☐ allocating some of the disabled person's duties to another employee

Chartered Institute of Personnel and Development

Customer Satisfaction Survey

*We would be grateful if you could spend a few minutes answering these questions and return the postcard to CIPD. <u>Please use a black pen to answer</u>. **If you would like to receive a free CIPD pen, please include your name and address.*** IPD MEMBER Y/N

....

1. Title of book ....

2. Date of purchase: month .... year ....

3. How did you acquire this book?
☐ Bookshop   ☐ Mail order   ☐ Exhibition ☐ Gift   ☐ Bought from Author

4. If ordered by mail, how long did it take to arrive:
☐ 1 week   ☐ 2 weeks   ☐ more than 2 weeks

5. Name of shop .... Town.. Country............

6. Please grade the following according to their influence on your purchasing decision with 1 as least influential: (please tick)

	1	2	3	4	5
Title					
Publisher					
Author					
Price					
Subject					
Cover					

7. On a scale of 1 to 5 (with 1 as poor & 5 as excellent) please give your impressions of the book in terms of: (please tick)

	1	2	3	4	5
Cover design					
Paper/print quality					
Good value for money					
General level of service					

8. Did you find the book:
Covers the subject in sufficient depth   ☐ Yes   ☐ No
Useful for your work   ☐ Yes   ☐ No

9. Are you using this book to help:
☐ In your work ☐ Personal study   ☐ Both   ☐ Other (please state)

Please complete if you are using this as part of a course

10. Name of academic institution..

11. Name of course you are following? ....

12. Did you find this book relevant to the syllabus? ☐ Yes ☐ No ☐ Don't know

Thank you!

To receive regular information about CIPD books and resources call 020 8263 3387.

Any data or information provided to the CIPD for the purposes of membership and other Institute activities will be processed by means of a computer database or otherwise. You may, from time to time, receive business information relevant to your work from the Institute and its other activities. If you do not wish to receive such information please write to the CIPD, giving your full name, address and postcode. The Institute does not make its membership lists available to any outside organisation.

1795/05/00

2 1

BUSINESS REPLY SERVICE
Licence No WD 1019

Publishing Department

Chartered Institute of Personnel and Development

CIPD House

Camp Road

Wimbledon

London

SW19 4BR

☐ transferring the disabled person to fill an existing vacancy
☐ altering the disabled person's working hours
☐ assigning the disabled person to a different place of work
☐ allowing the disabled person to be absent during working hours for rehabilitation, assessment, or treatment.

This list is not exhaustive, however, and in the case of *London Borough of Hillingdon* v *Morgan*,[49] involving an employee suffering from myalgic encephalomyelitis (ME), it was considered that a reasonable adjustment would have been to allow the employee temporarily to work from home.

Employers who without justification fail to comply with the duty in relation to a disabled person are taken to have discriminated against that person, and therefore an employer who dismisses an employee absent because of a stress-related illness without taking the sort of steps described in section 6(3) is vulnerable to claims of unlawful discrimination.

Pension provisions

Certain occupations, for example the emergency services, provide for the payment of enhanced pensions if employees are injured in the execution of their duties. Two cases in particular show clearly that the law's recognition of workplace stress is moving forward in this area also.

Former PC Bob Pickering, who joined the police force in 1971, was forced to retire some 20 years later suffering from a depressive illness.[50] He had been continually involved in violent confrontations while processing prisoners remanded in custody and in 1988 suffered a permanent injury to his shoulder as a result of being attacked by an individual. Three years later he was beaten up by another prisoner who escaped into the street from the local magistrates' court. He testified that:

> I became increasingly nervous, was tense all the time and dreaded going to work. I would go to bed sweating and get up at four in the morning. I would have crying fits. I lost my confidence and dreaded going back to work after the weekends.

The Police Pensions Regulations 1987 provide for payment of an enhanced pension if:

a policeman...is disabled as a result of an injury received without his own default in the execution of his duty.[51]

On balance, the Crown Court (hearing his appeal from the Sussex Police Authority) was satisfied that his depressive illness caused by the stress of his duties was an 'injury' sustained in the line of his duty and had led to his disablement.

In a similar case under the Firemen's Pension Scheme a retired fireman won his claim to have his depression treated as a 'disease' entitling him to an injury award under the scheme (*Bradley* v *London Fire and Civil Defence Authority*).[52] It provided for an award where:

a regular firefighter who is retired...is permanently disabled as a result of an infirmity occasioned by an injury (including disease)...received without his own default in the execution of his duty.[53]

Such decisions are important because they may well lead to many similar cases, and because the claims are in some respects easier to establish than a personal injury claim. There is no requirement in these regulations to prove 'foreseeability' of psychiatric harm, or that the employer failed in the duty of care. The only relevant issues will be whether the individual has suffered an 'injury', and whether the causation requirement is satisfied – in other words, whether it has been shown that the injury was sustained 'in the execution of duty'.

Criminal injuries compensation

Strictly speaking, it is not correct to include the criminal injuries compensation scheme in this chapter, because it is a publicly funded scheme rather than one that imposes liability on employers. Nevertheless, it may be worth pointing out that, although the scheme compensates only those who suffer an injury as a result of a crime of violence, the term 'injury' encompasses both mental and physical injury. It may thus provide a useful alternative to civil action to, for example, building society or other retail staff involved in a hold-up or other violent incident who suffer shock. Under the scheme, 'shock' is stated to include PTSD, depression and other related psychological symptoms. (See Appendix 3; but note that the tariff system introduced in April 1994 has been successfully challenged in the courts, and until a new scheme is introduced there is therefore no fixed sum for particular injuries.) It specifically includes railway workers who suffer shock through witnessing the injury or death of trespassers on the railway.

As in the case of pension provisions, causation must be satisfied, but there is no foreseeability requirement.

Summary

Workplace stress is not only an issue in relation to personal injury actions. It is also relevant to:

☐ criminal liability under HASAWA and other related health and safety legislation (maximum penalty if tried in Magistrates' Court is £20,000 and up to six months' imprisonment; if tried in Crown Court the fine is unlimited and up to two years' imprisonment)

☐ liability for awards of unfair dismissal compensation (maximum £6,900 basic award, calculated as for statutory redundancy payment, and £50,000 compensatory award)

☐ liability for awards of compensation for unlawful discrimination under the SDA, RRA and the DDA (unlimited awards)

☐ enhanced pension payments under specific pension schemes

☐ awards under the Criminal Injuries Compensation Scheme.

References

1 HSE. *Stress at Work: A guide for employers*. Suffolk, HSE Books, 1995 (available from HMSO).
2 [1983] ICR 257.
3 Cox T. *Stress Research and Stress Management: Putting theory to work*. HSE Contract Research Report No 61/1993, Suffolk, HSE Books, 1993.
4 [1984] IRLR 93.
5 *The Times*. 'Detective who lost her baby awarded £15,000'. 21 August 1995.
6 [1994] IRLR 384.
7 [1980] IRLR 340.
8 [1988] IRLR 510.

9 [1977] ICR 566.

10 Case No. 59097/93.

11 [1980] IRLR 53.

12 [1991] IRLR 309.

13 [1972] ICR 101.

14 [1976] IRLR 376.

15 [1990] IRLR 164.

16 [1999] IRLR 77817

17 [1978] ICR 221.

18 [1981] IRLR 347.

19 Case No. 00630/92.

20 Case No. 23299/91.

21 Case No. 13075/93.

22 'A person discriminates against a woman...if on the ground of her sex he treats her less favourably than he treats or would treat a man.'

23 By virtue of section 3(1) of the RRA 'racial grounds' means on grounds of colour, race, nationality, or ethnic or national origins (and a racial group is a group of persons similarly defined).

24 [1990] IRLR 288.

25 [1992] IRLR 257.

26 [1992] IRLR 259.

27 Earnshaw J. M. and Davidson M. J. 'Remedying sexual harassment via industrial tribunal claims: an investigation of the legal and psychosocial process'. *Personnel Review*. Vol. 23(8). pp3-16. 1994.

28 [1997] IRLR 168.

29 Case No 38395/96.

30 [1996] IRLR 596.

31 [1988] IRLR 190.

32 [1993] IRLR 445.

33 EOR. 'Taking the cap off discrimination awards'. *Equal Opportunities Review*. No. 57. September/October 1994.

34 EOR. 'Compensation awards '98 – a record year'. *Equal Opportunities Review*. No 86. July/August 1999.

35 Case No. 53435/93.

36 Case No. 2801882/97.

37 Case No. 7575/95.

38 Case No. 2300435/98.

39 Case No. 2800894/96.

40 Case No. 56617/94.

41 *Sherriff* v *Klyne Tugs (Lowestoft) Ltd* [1999] IRLR 481.

42 [1979] IRLR 127.

43 [1992] IRLR 251.

44 Those employing fewer than 15 employees are excluded from the Act.

45 [1999] IRLR 4.

46 There is no statutory definition of 'substantial adverse effect', but the Guidance states that a 'substantial' effect is one that is more than minor or trivial. [Para A1]

47 [1999] IRLR 14.

48 Quoted in Doyle B. *Disability Discrimination: The new law*. Bristol, Jordan, 1996.

49 Case No 1493/98.

50 *Daily Mail*. 'PC who found the stress too much wins his "injury claim"'. 27 May 1995.

51 Section B3, S.I. 1987, No. 257.

52 [1995] IRLR 46.

53 Firemen's Pension Scheme Order 1992: rule A9, B4.

6 THE SURVEYS AND THE CASE STUDIES

Introduction

Prior to the decision in the *Walker* case (see Chapter 4), there had been speculation and rumour for some considerable time that claims arising out of workplace stress would inevitably occur or might even be in the pipeline. A short questionnaire sent to just under 200 personal injury solicitors in early 1994 confirmed this to be the case. Only 48 replies were received, but 14 of these answered positively to the question:

> Has your firm been involved in the last five years in a personal injury claim in which workplace stress was the cause of the injury or a contributory factor?

Several solicitors also indicated a willingness to be interviewed or supplied details of cases in which they were involved; these provided the basis for most of the case studies outlined below. All provide powerful illustrations of key themes which remain just as relevant today.

In 1995 a further survey of personal injury solicitors revealed a clearer picture of the nature of ongoing claims, the sorts of jobs affected and the factors alleged to cause the injury.

The 1995 survey

The survey carried out in 1995 targeted 400 personal injury firms and got a response rate of just over 21 per cent. The results confirmed suspicions raised by the earlier survey: John Walker's case may have been the first successful stress-related personal injury claim, but it is unlikely to be the last. Out of 85 firms that returned questionnaires, 17 indicated that they were involved in a workplace stress claim.

It might have been predicted that the publicity surrounding the Walker case would have spawned a number of similar cases in the public sector. However, this was not the actual outcome: there was an even split between the public and the private sectors, and claimants included members of the police force, sales staff, a health worker, driver, manager, refuse collector, kitchen assistant, social worker, headteacher, soldier and cleaner.

Following the same argument, it was expected that most cases would involve work overload or long working hours. Again this proved not to be the case. A worrying finding was that by far the most prevalent trigger for the stress injury was alleged to be bullying in one shape or another (sometimes described as persecution, victimisation or pressure management).

The most common 'injury' reported was either a 'nervous breakdown' or depression, although mention was also made of suicide, asthma, death, PTSD, hypertension and diabetes.

The picture that emerged from this fairly unsophisticated survey was that workplace stress cannot be shrugged off as something relatively trivial or arising only in recognisably stressful jobs. It was clear that some employees were suffering significant psychiatric harm allegedly brought about not only by generalised overwork but, in many cases, by targeted behaviour in the form of victimisation or bullying. A wide variety of jobs was involved and, given the predominance of bullying or similar behaviour, it is perhaps not surprising to find that it was not particularly jobs at senior management level that were affected. Perhaps the greater degree of autonomy and control over their work is what makes such workers less vulnerable; conversely, the lack of it is a key factor in producing stress.

Although the survey showed that workplace stress claims were ongoing, surprisingly few of them have led to a reported outcome. As noted in Chapter 1, there have been some fairly substantial out-of-court settlements, but no additional case law that would help employers to be clearer about what is currently expected of them. It was therefore decided to conduct further research to investigate why these personal injury claims were not coming to court.

The 1998 survey

As in the earlier surveys, the investigation began with a questionnaire sent to personal injury solicitors, but in the event it was the follow-up interviews that provided the real clues to the realities of workplace stress claims. First and foremost, it was universally acknowledged by solicitors that the issue of funding is problematic, given the difficulty of obtaining union backing and the demise of legal aid. Although conditional fee arrangements[1] are now possible, interviewees felt that, before entering into such an arrangement, an accurate assessment of risk in the case was essential. This in itself entails an initial investigation likely to cost in the region of £1,000.

If and when a claim did get off the ground, the principal difficulty for the employee appeared to be satisfying the 'foreseeability' criterion, ie that the employer knew or ought to have known of the risk to the employee's psychological health. The most common problem was the lack of proper documentation to support the employee's claim, partly because of a reluctance on their part to inform the employer of the true nature of their medical condition. However, lack of accurate documentation also made life problematic for employers who had to defend claims. Having to rely on oral evidence from witnesses was regarded as fraught with difficulty on all sides.

Solicitors recognised the problems surrounding the issue of causation. If initial investigation of the claim revealed, for example, a bereavement shortly before the 'injury' in question or a previous episode of psychiatric ill-health, it could be hard to show that work was indeed the cause of the injury. However, if employers were aware of any such 'vulnerability', this could also work against them, because it would then be easier to argue that they should have foreseen the risk to the employee in question.

The case studies

The situations presented here are *not based on facts as determined in a court of law* or as a result of some investigation by management. They are simply the stories as told by aggrieved employees either to their solicitor or, sometimes, directly to us. In that sense they are nothing more than allegations. However, that does not mean that they should be dismissed out of hand – for several reasons. Firstly, whether true or false, they represent a situation in which, by reason of events in the workplace, individuals are left with strong feelings of resentment, anger or indignation. Secondly, whatever the rights and wrongs, it appears that the health of these individuals has been detrimentally affected, in some cases quite severely. Their stories are therefore presented as if they were factually correct.

Work overload

Facts

Mrs A was a social worker. By 1988 she had obtained a position as team leader working for the social services department of a local authority. The area for which she was responsible had a high statutory caseload (ie children subject to care or supervision orders) and a substantial child-abuse referral rate. Mrs A's team was understaffed, and team leaders such as Mrs A had to attend child-protection conferences and cases in the High Court.

In January 1989 Mrs A, having been in pain for some time, saw a consultant, who diagnosed irritable bowel syndrome caused mainly by stress. However, she continued to work, assisted by medication, and took time off only when in extreme pain. In October 1989, as a consequence of financial restraints, there was a freeze on vacant posts, and Mrs A lost three social workers from her team. This resulted in a number of statutory cases not being visited and Mrs A having to make decisions about the priority of cases, all of which were in urgent need of attention. Mrs A asked for work to be sent to other teams, but when a team with which she was on friendly terms agreed to accept some of her workload, the union stepped in and refused to allow this course of action.

In December 1989 Mrs A had a supervision session with her area manager, in the course of which he commented adversely on her sickness record. Mrs A said:

> I blew up at him, making it quite clear the pressure that I was under and how I came in even when I was unwell...I do not recall any offer of help resulting from that meeting, even though I made it quite clear about the pressure.

In fact Mrs A complained to her area manager throughout the

period of the freeze on vacant posts, and encouraged others to do the same.

In March 1990 the freeze was lifted but Mrs A had still not reached her full complement of social workers by June 1990, when she was diagnosed by her GP as suffering from stress. She felt sick all the time and was constantly tired. Mrs A was off work until November 1990, during which time the local authority paid for counselling sessions. When she returned to work she was offered a different job, one that involved rewriting procedures. It required her to be confident, to show initiative and to work alone, none of which she was capable of doing at that time. Added to this she was placed in an office with a member of staff with whom she had been in conflict the previous year. She complained about this, but nothing was done. Mrs A became depressed to the point that when, in January 1991, she broke her arm and was off work, she simply could not face going back. Ultimately, following a psychiatrist's report, she was retired in 1991.

Outcome

In September 1991 Mrs A signed on for a one-year MA course but suffered bouts of illness. 'It was as if my immune system had broken down', she said. Following the course she was unemployed until March 1993, when she obtained work with the probation service. The work was part time, and Mrs A found that, although she was asked to do extra hours occasionally, she could not sustain that higher level of work indefinitely. She could no longer cope with pressure. As an example of her inability to cope she recounted that, in September 1992, she could not handle her then 12-year-old daughter's 'typical teenager' behaviour and felt compelled to place her in a boarding school. As a result of this financial commitment Mrs A got into debt and obtained legal aid with a view to suing her local authority. She says:

> I feel that I have been robbed of a career that I loved, which has had a great emotional and distressing effect upon me.

Comment

Mrs A's case bears a passing resemblance to Mr Walker's (see Chapter 4), but there are some notable differences:

☐ Although Mrs A contracted irritable bowel syndrome in 1989, it is not clear precisely what 'illness' led to her retirement in 1991.

☐ There does not appear to be any suggestion that she complained of her workload prior to January 1989. Even though Mr Walker did complain prior to his first breakdown, it was still held to be unforeseeable, so it seems unlikely in the extreme that the council could be held responsible for Mrs A's irritable bowel syndrome.

☐ In relation to the events leading up to her final retirement, the most striking difference about Mrs A's situation is that the council actually did do something to assist, namely by placing her in an alternative job. Thus, in addition to establishing an 'injury' caused by the workplace that was reasonably foreseeable, Mrs A also needed to show that this was not sufficient to satisfy the duty of care.

Hostility/persecution

Facts

Mr B returned to teaching in a school in northern England after taking six years out to spend time in industry. He returned to find himself teamed with a head of department 10 years younger than himself; he subsequently endured a period of eight years of hostility and persecution. Mr B stated:

> For eight years I have been on guard not to make a wrong move. For eight years he has not flagged in his hostility, which is the more baffling because he is charming and helpful to everyone else. Ours is a secret, deadly struggle.

His concerns can be conveniently classified under three main headings:

1 Lack of consultation
  ☐ no departmental meetings
  ☐ change of textbooks throughout the school without consultation
  ☐ giving Mr B the largest and most difficult classes to teach
  ☐ refusal to give a detailed syllabus, with the result that Mr B's pupils did badly in internal exams set by the head of department

□ textbooks removed from classroom without notification, with the result that when Mr B came to use them they were not there
□ all initiatives or suggestions vetoed with the statement, 'I'm in charge'
□ departmental outings arranged in secret, ensuring that Mr B was excluded.

2 Failure to communicate information
□ no information provided about budget
□ where possible, exam results withheld
□ departmental magazines, periodicals, etc never passed on
□ information about meetings passed on too late for Mr B to attend.

3 Persecution
□ by word and attitude conveyed continuous dissatisfaction with Mr B's teaching
□ in a school reorganisation strove to have him replaced by a teacher later dismissed for incompetence
□ heard in staffroom openly advocating Mr B's dismissal
□ when giving instructions frequently referred to the amount of money Mr B was being paid to obey orders
□ Mr B could never be absent because he knew his cupboards and books would be gone through.

Outcome

Over the years Mr B spoke several times to two headteachers and a deputy head about the matter. They were not unsympathetic, but no action was ever taken, because they were reluctant to cross the individual concerned. The strain of being in a constant state of anxiety, resentment and anger took a physical toll. Mr B lost two stone in weight. Each morning, as he drove to work, he would develop a vicious pain in the back. Headaches were a daily occurrence. He found himself sleeping alternate nights: the first night alert because of worry, the second night asleep because of exhaustion. Some respite has come in recent years because he is now teaching exam classes up to A level, and results show that his competence as a teacher can no longer be questioned. The conflict with his head of department remains, however, a bitter experience, especially as the head of department is on record as having driven another teacher to talk of suicide and eventually into retiring.

Comment

As yet Mr B may not have suffered a recognisable psychiatric condition that would enable him to pursue a personal injury claim. Nevertheless, were he to leave and claim constructive dismissal, it is arguable that his employer, by failing to respond to his complaints and provide him with support, is in breach of the implied term of his contract relating to mutual trust and confidence. Alternatively, Mr B could argue a breach of the implied term that the employer take reasonable care for his health and safety.

Bullying/pressure management

Facts

Mr C started work for X Co as an engineer and was later promoted to deputy shift manager. During 1992, while he was seconded to work in France, the company won a contract to supply goods for Z Co. In January 1993 Mr C returned to the UK to find that the company was experiencing several problems and, in particular, that Z Co was demanding extreme standards in quality and supply. These supply demands led to planned maintenance not being carried out; in consequence, mechanical failures occurred and there was frustration at both shopfloor and top management level. Some weeks later, fearing the loss of the contract with Z Co, head office at X Co decided to send in a team of five US trouble-shooters, whose job responsibilities subsequently fluctuated because of the turmoil at the plant.

Towards the end of March 1993 the plant manager went off sick as a result of the pressures, and was replaced by another American. Working hours were increased and days off were cancelled to 'help the plant out'. Originally there had been four shift managers operating 8am to 8pm and 8pm to 8am shifts, but in May 1993 one of them resigned on the spot after being verbally abused by Mr D, one of the Americans. Mr C was then asked to step in and take his place, but he was reluctant to do so; he did eventually agree, but only after several discussions with one of the personnel managers.

In Mr C's words, 'From the end of April '93 the trouble-shooters were beginning to flex their muscles hard and the shift managers were the bearers of it all.' Mr C felt that he and the other shift managers were unreasonably taken to task about absenteeism, safety and morale as the increased pressure on the workforce led to more accidents and higher levels of sickness absence.

Despite the pressure, production was not improving, and it remained difficult to achieve the quality demanded by Z Co, even though other customers were satisfied. Verbal abuse, intimidation and belittling of staff by the Americans, and in particular by Mr D, became a regular feature of working life. Mr D was at that time staying in a hotel adjoining a nightclub; on most nights, after returning to his room between 1am and 3am, he would phone into work and ask how the plant was running. If the answer was 'Not very well', he would rant and rave at the particular shift manager to whom he was speaking in such terms as these:

> I am going to fire you in the morning. What will your wife think about that: no new clothes or nice perfumes ever again. You are shit, you are.

The shift manager would then have to carry on running his shift with the fear that by 8am he would have no job. Even if that did not happen, the managers could be required to attend a 'morning meeting' until any time up till 10.30am, during which their overnight decisions would be questioned and discredited. As Mr C said, 'More confidence- and morale-bashing.'

Mr C and the other shift managers constantly complained about the trouble-shooters' intimidation, but because their organisation roles varied it was often difficult to know whom to complain to. On one occasion Mr C and his assistant went to see the replacement plant manager about the problem, but his response on this and subsequent occasions was only 'I will have a word with them.' Mr C's perception was that few dared to criticise the Americans because they had been sent from head office in the USA.

Outcome

On occasions Mr C began to contemplate suicide; following an incident of verbal abuse and intimidation by Mr D at the end of November 1993, Mr C reluctantly visited his doctor. The doctor diagnosed 'debility' and recommended Mr C to refrain from working. When Mr C protested that he never took time off work, his GP's response was that, unless he did so, he 'would not be working much longer'. Two weeks later, two other shift managers went off sick with 'psychiatric illnesses', although they returned to work in early 1994. By this time head office in the UK began to realise that there was a problem and sent Mr D back to the USA.

When Mr C had been off work for three months a doctor retained by the company visited him at home. He told Mr C that he was:

> fed up with telling this company about how they operate . . . they will kill someone before long. I am going to report back that you have had a serious nervous breakdown.

This doctor is no longer retained by the company but, following his report, Mr C was sent by the company to a psychiatrist. He was treated for six months by this psychiatrist, who then recommended a probable return to work, though not in the same environment, in 12 months' time. However, by September 1995 both an independent GP representing the Department of Social Security (DSS) and a second psychiatrist to whom Mr C was referred by the company had expressed the opinion that he was not ready for work. While remaining in the company's employ, Mr C instigated legal proceedings in respect of his breakdown.

Comment

Both the company doctor and the first psychiatrist to whom Mr C was referred appeared to be convinced that Mr C had suffered a nervous breakdown. To establish that this was caused by his working environment was potentially easier than in the case of some of the employees discussed later in this chapter because Mr C was not, apparently, the only shift manager to be absent with a stress-related illness. Moreover, it was brought to his notice that a shift manager at one of the company's sister plants also suffered a nervous breakdown at a time (before November 1993) when their plant was under pressure.

Several factors appear to be relevant in this case in determining whether or not Mr C's breakdown was foreseeable. Firstly, it could be argued that, because of the experience of the shift manager at the sister plant, the company should have known what was likely to happen to shift managers in general in its employ when the pressure was on (even if the illnesses of the other shift managers at Mr C's plant are not relevant because they occurred after Mr C's absence began). Secondly, Mr C's complaints of victimisation should have put the company on notice of how the managers were being treated, although this would not of itself have indicated to management that the men were at risk of breakdown. If the company doctor had indeed warned X Co about its treatment of its workforce, then clearly his evidence would be crucial.

So far as the abusive and intimidatory behaviour of Mr D is concerned, it could be argued that his night-time telephone calls to the plant were not done 'in the course of employment' and thus the company was not liable for them. However, it seems equally arguable that, because the calls related to the running of the plant, and because Mr D was apparently in a position of authority over the shift managers, they were simply an unauthorised means of carrying out authorised managerial responsibility. In any case, Mr C believed he could establish that Mr D's aggression was well-known throughout the industry; if this were indeed so, then in allowing him free rein at their plant, X Co would be directly – as opposed to vicariously – liable for any breach of the duty of care. (NB This claim was subsequently settled for an undisclosed sum.)

Stressful working conditions and poor management style

Facts

Mr E was engaged for all of his working life in the repair and testing of electric rotating machinery. He was a conscientious employee who took a keen interest in his work and came to be regarded as one of the most accomplished electrical/mechanical fitters in the Manchester area. In 1969 he was recruited by a company based in the south of England that had been seeking to establish a foothold in the north-west and had eventually succeeded in buying out a firm in the region. A manager sent from the London branch indicated to Mr E that he was supervisor material and constantly assured him of his value to the company.

Before long, however, Mr E began to have misgivings. He realised that the standard and ability of many of the other tradesmen was poor, while he was himself being subjected to long spells of working seven days a week. As a conscientious worker he acquiesced in a regime that detrimentally affected his home life; this was because the company emphasised how vital a role he was playing while it acquired more trained men and established itself on a firm footing.

Some months later the manager sent for his assistant from the Southampton branch. Mr E soon realised that this individual lacked both training and ability, and that he compensated for his limitations by adopting an abusive style of management and by speaking almost exclusively in expletives. When the men requested an extractor fan to remove the black smog being produced by the burning-off of rancid transformer oil, the assistant's reaction was, 'If they don't like it, tell them they can have their cards. I could get monkeys to do their jobs.'

Meanwhile the drive to recruit new staff had continued to the point that the men were working in impossibly cramped conditions. Because many of the recruits had little knowledge of the work, the men started to question the judgement of the managers, and morale became affected. It took a further knock in 1971 with the arrival of a second outsider, who was sent from the Birmingham branch to be the foreman. His response to the greeting proffered by Mr E was, 'You are all a load of savages up here.'

Mr E began to perceive a growing feeling of militancy among the men, mainly among those who could actually do their jobs. It also seemed to him that others coped by being sycophantic, for example by socialising with management outside working hours, and that this gained them promotion. In effect, a split emerged between those who continued to be given impossible workloads and those who were 'in' with management and given sinecures and light duties. Some individuals were loaned money by the company and encouraged to buy houses or cars; others became bitterly resentful, which resulted in walkouts and stoppages.

Several men eventually had breakdowns; Mr E's job satisfaction plummeted. He commented:

> From an occupation I had enjoyed for years, taking deep interest in my work, every day became an endurance and I was just going through the motions through fatigue and low morale.

In 1974 he himself suffered a nervous breakdown, and his specialist gave instructions that in the future he should not do excessive overtime. In fact, when Mr E returned to work, the manager gave instructions that he was to do no overtime at all. (This terrified other workers who had gained large mortgages on the basis of vast amounts of overtime: they wondered if the same thing might happen to them.) By the following year the wage bill of the company could not be supported by the profit margin, and Mr E was made redundant.

Outcome

Mr E subsequently managed to form his own highly successful company, but by 1979 he had begun to develop angina. He then underwent a heart triple by-pass operation; ultimately he suffered a massive coronary which left him with a large area of his heart permanently damaged. In 1983, at the age of 47, he was forced to retire from his company, and his working life ended. His income now consists of invalidity benefit and mobility allowance; he still suffers from angina, and he takes medication such as beta-blockers and anticoagulants. He says he realises that:

> the adverse effects of stress are not just about long hours or even hard work, but are caused mainly by utter frustration – where people feel that their working life and pride have been taken from them, and they are unable to do anything about it.

Comment

It was only when reading an article in 1994 about stress litigation that Mr E realised there could be any redress for damage to health caused by undue stress at work. Despite this he has not seen a solicitor, for two reasons: first, because he would not be able to afford legal fees and, secondly, because of the 20-year time lapse since he worked for the company. The Limitation Act

1980 as amended by the Latent Damage Act 1986 provides that in the case of actions in negligence where the damage claimed is in respect of personal injury, the limitation period is three years (for further detail, see Chapter 8). Had Mr E taken action at the time he would no doubt have been faced with the same problem of foreseeability discussed in earlier case studies. He would also have had difficulty establishing that the coronary, if not the breakdown, was caused by his working environment rather than being something that would have happened anyway. Nevertheless, Mr E is firmly of the view that:

> my health was seriously and permanently damaged by being employed by a company where injustice, malpractices and even corruption was rife.

Persecution

Facts

At the age of 53, Mr F was appointed to the post of secretary and general manager of an organisation (Benvo) set up for benevolent purposes and managed by an executive committee. One aspect of Benvo's activities was the ownership and operation of a residential accommodation in Blankshire known as Restho. Mr F was responsible to the executive committee for the management and financial accounting of Restho. He had a good working relationship with the chairman of the committee and, so far as he was aware, he was in good health. However, when this chairman retired, his deputy, Mr G, took over. According to Mr F, Mr G and the outgoing chairman had never been on good terms, and Mr F's only explanation for his subsequent treatment by Mr G was a resentment by Mr G of the relationship between Mr F and Mr G's predecessor.

Only two months after his appointment as chairman, Mr G visited Restho and, without any prior investigation, falsely accused Mr F of selling certain property belonging to Benvo and stealing the proceeds. The allegations were repeated to another member of the executive committee and to employees who were subordinate to Mr F. Moreover, Mr G refused either to withdraw them or to investigate the books, which would have shown that the proceeds of sale of the property had been credited to Benvo. Mr F wrote a formal letter of grievance to Mr G and stated that the incident had caused him stress. Mr G made no response to the letter.

Subsequently Mr G embarked on a series of actions designed to undermine Mr F's position and authority. In particular he appointed his stepson to a trainee post at Restho to act as a secret informer who would gather information about Mr F's doings. Mr F had no idea that the person appointed was Mr G's stepson, but he did subsequently suspect that someone close to him was stirring up matters. Mr G also repeatedly refused to sanction actions that Mr F felt to be necessary in view of the deteriorating financial position of Benvo. At some stage Mr F began to develop high blood pressure, and later also severe and recurring nosebleeds, of which his employers were aware.

As a result of an incident during which Mr F's authority over his subordinates was challenged, he compiled a situation report and sent it to Mr G. In it he outlined the deliberate undermining of his position and the stress he was suffering. He also had conversations with Mr G and the other members of the executive committee to the same effect. Mr G's response was to swear at Mr F and verbally abuse him, and subsequently the following took place:

☐ Mr G sent Mr F a letter making false accusations against him and threatening unspecified action.

☐ A little less than a month later, Mr G wrote to Mr F demanding an explanation about the number of staff who had left or been dismissed in the preceding three years. Mr F responded that most had been temporary trainees and gave a proper explanation in respect of the others.

☐ At a meeting between the two men Mr G threatened and intimidated Mr F.

☐ Immediately prior to a meeting of the executive committee, Mr G handed to Mr F a letter itemising 19 allegations against him in relation to his work, supposedly compiled from hand-written complaints by Mr F's immediate subordinates. Mr G refused to produce the hand-written complaints, and an inquiry into the matter set up by the committee found none of the complaints to be substantiated.

☐ Mr G summoned Mr F's subordinates to the committee meeting and required a hand-written report from each of them regarding the state of Restho and any complaints they wished to raise. None of them produced any such report.

- Mr F was summoned by Mr G to a meeting of six to eight members of the committee, plus Mr F's subordinates – a meeting that Mr F described as a 'kangaroo court'. He stood at one end of a long table and, as Mr G pointed to each member of the meeting in turn, was subjected to a barrage of orchestrated and fabricated accusations. Mr F, feeling as if he were dreaming, was given no opportunity to reply and left the meeting saying that he felt unwell.

- Shortly afterwards Mr G came to Mr F's office and demanded his resignation in writing. He informed him that if he did not resign, he (Mr G) would dismiss him. To this effect he told Mr F's secretary to type out a letter of dismissal which he would later sign (Mr F was in fact dismissed about a month and a half later). During this incident Mr F was visibly unwell.

Outcome

Over the weekend following the 'kangaroo court' meeting, Mr F suffered blurring vision and became increasingly unwell. On the Monday morning he consulted his GP and was urgently referred to a consultant. His blood pressure reading on that day was 210/130, a level which his consultant regarded as 'not just a risk to health but a severe threat to his life'. Mr F was later diagnosed as having sustained PTSD and a thrombosis of an artery of his left eye, which (by reducing the vision by 80 per cent) effectively rendered him blind in that eye. The condition was regarded as incurable and Mr F also began to experience blurring of vision in his right eye brought on by the strain and overuse of the right eye. According to his Statement of Claim, he suffered from:

> excessive tiredness, depression, frustration and mood swings, nightmares and reduced ability to participate in normal social and leisure activities. He cannot comfortably watch television, or read a newspaper or book for longer than a few minutes and has difficulty playing snooker and golf and performing household tasks. His normal domestic life has been severely impaired in quality by his changed personality and loss of capabilities.

Mr F was told that he was unlikely to be fit for work before reaching the age of 65. A personal injury claim was commenced against Benvo.

Comment

If Mr G was indeed 'out to get' Mr F, then this is an appalling case. There is a clear diagnosis of both physical and psychiatric injury, and the consultant's report notes that Mr F had 'been subjected to long-duration stressors prior to acute major stressors [at executive committee and in the 'kangaroo court'] . . . There is no evidence that [he] suffered from any psychological or psychiatric disturbances prior to [that].' The finding of a DSS adjudication officer that the injury to Mr F's eye was an 'industrial accident' (ie arising out of and in the course of employment) provides further confirmation that Mr F's condition was caused by events at work.

It also appears that foreseeability might be easier to establish here than in some of the other case histories, on account of the two situation reports written by Mr F stating that he found the events which were the subject of the reports stressful. Evidence is apparently also available from Mr F's assistant to the effect that, around the time of the two key meetings, he was offered Mr F's job on the basis that Mr F needed to be replaced because he was ill. It will be interesting to see whether courts will view the question of foreseeability differently where harm is inflicted intentionally, or whether they will simply view the plaintiff's case in a more favourable light.

Mr G is now dead. In the circumstances, unless Benvo had some strong evidence to counter Mr F's version of events, they might well prefer to settle out of court, given the embarrassment that could be caused by the revelation of Mr F's allegations in the public arena.

Failure to provide counselling

Facts

Mr H was employed by a local authority from 1975 until 1989 in their emergency services department. In the course of his employment he was placed in life-threatening situations, subjecting him to great fear, and was required to deal with violent incidents and attempted suicides. He also observed dead and mutilated bodies.

Outcome

Mr H allegedly developed PTSD in the late 1970s, initially having nightmares about his work and experiencing more severe and persistent symptoms as time went by. In 1988 he went absent from work owing to depression and was medically retired in November 1989. Subsequently he instructed solicitors to act for him against his employers, alleging that if counselling had been made available he would not have suffered depression in the way he had and would therefore not have lost his employment. A consultant psychiatrist to whom he was referred diagnosed PTSD arising out of his employment, which 'may have been ameliorated or prevented with appropriate counselling'. The consultant also diagnosed depression which, in his view, was largely the consequence of the PTSD but was also partly attributable to various events in Mr H's personal life in the mid- to late 1980s. Legal opinion was that, on the medical evidence, Mr H might have difficulty persuading the court that:

☐ the PTSD was indeed attributable to work
☐ on the balance of probabilities he would not have suffered the PTSD and/or depression had counselling been provided.

It was also pointed out that his employers would not be in breach of duty unless by the early to mid-1980s it was either common practice among local authorities to make counselling available or, if not general practice, it was known that employees were exposed to horrific incidents and the likelihood that such employees would suffer psychological consequences was or should have been known and his employers knew or should have known that there was something they could do to reduce or prevent the likelihood of psychiatric illness.

When further investigation revealed that in the early to mid-1980s the psychological consequences of exposure to horrific incidents were not known to employers (ie until after such disasters as Zeebrugge and King's Cross), and that no counselling was given to members of emergency services until the mid- to late 1980s, a decision was taken not to pursue the claim further.

Comment

This case study emphasises two particular points made in

Chapter 4. The first is the importance of being able to establish causation (ie that the injury was caused by the employer's breach of duty) when employees have stresses outside the workplace as well as within it. It also highlights the point that the employer is judged by the state of knowledge at the time of the alleged breach of duty – in this case the early to mid-1980s. In the light of current awareness of PTSD and the benefits of providing counselling (see Chapter 7), Mr H's case might have taken a different course had the events taken place in a present-day workplace.

Stressful working conditions/failure to provide counselling

Facts

Mr J was employed in the prison service. During his initial training period he was instructed in suicide prevention and in physically controlling inmates in given situations, but not in dealing with his personal stress. At first he coped with the long and sometimes unpredictable working hours, although he found his duties exhausting and his holidays limited. He regarded himself as having been a happy-go-lucky individual when he joined the service.

As time went on Mr J found himself becoming more irritable, but it also seemed to him that senior staff were unconcerned about his welfare. He did not complain because, in his eyes, that would have had a detrimental effect on his progress. For years he kept a diary in which he recorded that he was regularly required to work more than 50 hours a week and that, in some weeks, his hours of work could reach 80. Mr J's wife remembers his working around 72 hours a week for at least three months, without a day off, in 1983; she can recall another similar period of six months during the same decade.

In the course of his duties Mr J was directly involved in such traumatic incidents as attempted suicides, when he would be required to render aid or even, for example, to attempt to resuscitate individuals who had hanged themselves. On occasions, would-be suicides slashed themselves; Mr J recollects a particular case which required him personally to put 156 stitches in the inmate's arms. On other occasions he was assaulted by inmates. No counselling was ever offered to him after such violent attacks or other traumatic events.

In 1986 Mr J had become a hospital officer and hence took responsibility for ensuring that prisoners who were prescribed medication actually took it. He was given an 'official' phone at home and, as a result, was often called in to deal with medical emergencies when the part-time doctor was unavailable. Sometimes it was difficult to contact a doctor to make the necessary decisions and diagnosis, which Mr J found intensely stressful.

Outcome

From about 1986, following a particularly violent attack, Mr J noticed his health begin to deteriorate and he took sickness absence. He felt that the doctor he saw was loath to record him as suffering from anxiety for fear of affecting Mr J's chances of promotion. Mr J became frightened of going to work, and the stress he was suffering affected his home life. His children would avoid him when they saw that he had come home upset; he became a heavy drinker, had difficulty sleeping and often could not eat during the day. Ultimately Mr J was prescribed tranquillisers and lost two and a half stone in weight. In 1989 he was referred to a consultant psychiatrist who concluded that he was not in a suitable medical condition to continue his work as a prison officer. In 1990, aged 48, he was retired on medical grounds suffering from PTSD – and decided to take legal action against his employer.

Comment

Unlike in the previous case study, there does not appear to be a problem of additional causative factors in Mr J's case. Although he saw two marriages end in divorce, there seems to be no suggestion that Mr J's domestic difficulties caused his illness; rather it was his work and working environment that caused both his medical symptoms and the consequent detriment to his family life and relationships within the family. (In fact, Mr J's present wife and his children also suffered stress-related symptoms that they attributed to his behaviour.) However, the issue of foreseeability does seem comparable with the case of Mr H: arguably, the only significant difference between the two men is that there was apparently a period of some four years during which Mr J's absence record gradually deteriorated. However, two additional factors weaken the contention that this should have put Mr J's employer on notice of his vulnerability to stress. The first is that it is not known what diagnosis was recorded by his doctor at the time. The second (which may be linked to the first) is that Mr J claims that he was conscious of people checking up on him when he was absent, so his absences may not have been regarded as genuine.

Regardless of questions of foreseeability and causation, success or failure for Mr J could turn simply on the fact that his 'injury' was sustained at the latest in 1990. A Limitation Act issue (see page 149) was set down for hearing, with its outcome to determine whether the case should proceed to trial.

Overwork/lack of support

Facts

In June 1994 Mr K, a salesman, was asked to cover additional areas, which necessitated extra travelling and working a 70-hour week. The response to his request for help was that surely he would not want the regional manager to hear that he could not cope; he himself feared that he would lose a particularly lucrative geographical sales area if he persisted with further requests. In the event a trainee was provided, but this proved more of a hindrance than a help, because the trainee constantly needed telling what to do.

By the time reinforcements were provided to reduce Mr K's workload the damage had been done and, in September, his GP prescribed beta-blockers in addition to other medication for stress. Owing to his state of exhaustion he could no longer engage in such leisure activities as football, and on one particular occasion he was sent home by the area trainer because he was not well enough to work. On learning that another employee had been offered stress management he once more appealed for help, only to be told that his situation was nothing in comparison.

Not surprisingly, Mr K's state of health affected his work performance. He was subjected to disciplinary proceedings over the state of his paperwork audit and subsequently dismissed.

Outcome

Mr K developed stomach and bowel problems and has now been

granted legal aid to pursue both unfair dismissal and a personal injury claim.

Comment

On the issue of foreseeability Mr K claimed that the regional manager had been briefed on the subject of stress and had been told by the sales director that anyone apparently suffering from it should be reported to him. It is also significant that stress management had allegedly been offered to at least one other member of staff. The company was thus aware, at least in general terms, that its workforce could be vulnerable to stress. However, establishing causation in Mr K's case was problematic because there were factors outside work that could equally well have caused (or at least contributed to) his illness. Firstly, he had moved house in April 1994. This of itself is generally regarded as a stressful event but, in addition, his new house needed major renovation. Secondly, Mr K's wife had been suffering from postnatal depression requiring medical treatment and, thirdly, there had been conflict between two sets of in-laws, leading to a lack of social support. On the other hand, if a court were to find that, but for the work situation, Mr K's health would not have broken down, knowledge of his domestic problems could be a relevant factor in assessing whether or not his employer had behaved reasonably in subjecting him to extra pressure at work.

Victimisation

Facts

Ms L, an academic member of staff of a university department, initiated employment tribunal proceedings, claiming victimisation on grounds of sex and of trade union activities. She alleged, among other things, that:

☐ her head of department refused her leave of absence which would have been necessary had she been successful in an application for a research fellowship. The application could not therefore be pursued.

☐ funding for her to attend the second year of a course approved as appropriate staff development was made conditional on her signing an undertaking to ensure that the department of which she was a member recouped its investment in terms of commitment to teaching in the subsequent two years. This was not normal practice.

□ she was told by her head of department that her application for conference funding could not be considered until she returned from sick leave (due to stress symptoms)

□ her head of department incorrectly told the director of undergraduate studies in a department in which Ms L provided a service course that she would be unable to teach the first session of the summer term because of a medical appointment. The session was cancelled and the department decided to use one of their own staff for the remainder of the course.

□ following disagreement between herself and other members of her subsection within the department, the head of department withdrew her from the subsection without giving her an opportunity to present her view of events.

□ it was orally agreed with her head of department that she would chair a particular working party. The following day he told her in a letter to stand down.

□ there was a failure to respond to her request on medical grounds for a car-parking space.

Outcome

Because the stress of the situation was affecting her health it was agreed that Ms L would move to another department. The process was carried out in a humiliating way and, although her discrimination claims were ultimately withdrawn, she resigned and moved to a different institution.

Comment

Ms L was fortunate in being able to remove herself from the stressful situation before her health was more severely affected. Because her claims were withdrawn we cannot know whether she was actually treated in the way she alleges either because she was a woman or because of her trade union activities. Her story should nevertheless send a warning to organisations about the potential consequences of what in fact may be a simple clash of personalities made more significant when one party is in a position of authority or power over the other.

Unsatisfactory system of work/working practices and procedure

Facts

Mr M had been successfully employed in a number of organisations but had no previous experience of the type of work he would be undertaking for his new employer. He had given particular attention, therefore, to the detailed discussion of his job description and training programme that had taken place at his interview. Almost immediately he started work, however, he was given additional duties not discussed at the interview – for example, line management responsibility for a number of his colleagues. Moreover, the training promised at the interview did not materialise; instead Mr M was sent on training courses that were either not relevant or took place only after the work for which they were intended to train Mr M had been completed.

More significantly, Mr M began experiencing problems with his own line manager. Communication between the two men was poor, and Mr M detected both a reluctance in his manager to explain his requirements and resentment when clarification was requested. As a result, Mr M felt that it was impossible to deliver work on time or plan his work effectively. As time went by he began to regard his line manager's behaviour as unreasonable, in that he:

☐ insisted that Mr M write a report about a computer system that did not exist

☐ 'moved the goalposts' by asking for a report about one thing but then, after Mr M had done the work, insisted he had asked for a report about something else

☐ rarely gave Mr M credit for his work

☐ frequently denigrated Mr M's work and talked sarcastically about it in front of others, to Mr M's embarrassment

☐ made trivial criticisms over such matters as full stops or spaces in internal memos

☐ cut passages out of reports without explanation, with the result that Mr M felt that a nonsense was being made of his work

☐ indulged in seemingly bizarre behaviour, such as remaining silent and ignoring questions put to him in meetings, whereas on other occasions he would talk incessantly and shout down Mr M when he spoke

□ spoke on occasions in a whining irate tone of voice similar to that of a sulking, angry child.

The behaviour of Mr M's manager was witnessed in meetings with senior managers; it also created conflict with other staff in Mr M's section, including those for whom he had line management responsibility. Four employees recruited to the section left within a year. Mr M unsuccessfully attempted to obtain proper work objectives and procedures by alerting his manager and others to the difficulties he was encountering. As the months passed, disagreements between Mr M and his manager became increasingly frequent, and when the latter began to cause distress to Mr M's direct report also, an approach was made to the head of department (Mr M's line manager's immediate superior). The outcome of this meeting was not satisfactory because, although the head of department revealed that the line manager suffered from epilepsy (which might have been the cause of his behaviour), she concluded following a meeting with him that there was no significant problem with his behaviour. In fact, she went so far as to suggest that it was Mr M's intention to cause trouble for his line manager.

The following month Mr M's responsibilities were changed without his being consulted, and he continued to feel that he was being deliberately mismanaged. He became increasingly stressed and, in due course, went onto long-term sick leave. Others in Mr M's section resigned at this time as a result of the unreasonable behaviour of Mr M's line manager. While on sick leave Mr M felt his psychological health further undermined by a 'performance review' in which it was suggested there had been a deterioration in his performance over a certain period, whereas a previous 'trial report' had recorded his performance as satisfactory. Moreover, the procedure for completing the performance review was not followed properly.

Outcome

In the event Mr M suffered a nervous breakdown necessitating psychotherapy, anti-depressants and anxiety-controlling drugs. He instructed a solicitor to take action against his employer, and counsel's opinion was sought as to the merits of the case.

Comment

Mr M spoke to several doctors and mental health workers in the area in which he was employed, each of whom apparently stated that his place of work was noted for cases of stress. It is claimed that some individuals had to be retired prematurely. If this was indeed the case and could be proved by reliable evidence, it would be a relevant factor in establishing foreseeability in Mr M's case. The consultant psychiatrist to whom Mr M was referred was of the opinion that his symptoms had arisen as a result of his working environment and not because of any medical condition existing prior to his employment. He also took the view that Mr M's feelings of persecution are not due to his being obsessive or having a 'paranoid personality disorder'. Depending on counsel's opinion, this is a case that could well proceed to trial – or be settled on the way.

Miscellaneous cases

The following are cases for which only brief details are given. This is because either the case was at an early stage, or a decision was taken not to pursue the claim, or full details were simply not available. Nevertheless they provide further illustration of the variety of occupations that may be vulnerable, and the ways in which claims may arise.

☐ A security guard was involved in a 'rationalisation' in which the company reduced employee numbers. The result was that there was no one to watch his back while he was emptying safes. There were lots of rules and regulations and the job was becoming more restrictive. In addition, there was apparently a vindictive manager who took pleasure in making people late in leaving work when he knew they had important commitments. Off work with stress, the security guard contacted a solicitor.

☐ A white-collar worker employed by a council had a nervous breakdown. However, he also had, as a local councillor, a heavy load outside work. The medical evidence could not establish that the breakdown was related to workplace conditions, and the case was dropped.

☐ A train driver killed a woman and two children, and brought a case based on the lack of counselling. Liability was admitted.

☐ A civil engineer who had a history of heart disease found his work intensified following job cuts. The employer was unaware of his pre-existing medical condition. Causation could not be established to a sufficient degree to make it worthwhile pursuing the case.

☐ An employee in the telecommunications industry was off work with stress. While at home he was telephoned by a manager, who allegedly made the original stress worse. The employee contacted a solicitor.

☐ A railway worker who warned management about a dangerous environment was sufficiently upset about the situation that he resigned, suffering from mild stress. About one year later the situation he had warned about came to pass and he suffered more serious psychiatric illness. He alleged that his employer was responsible.

☐ A market supervisor retired on medical grounds at age 40, having suffered a nervous breakdown. He engaged a solicitor, contending that the market had been run as a shambles, that the traders had ganged up on him and abused him, and that he had been given no management support. His solicitor initially commenced a constructive dismissal claim, but subsequently found the applicant extremely difficult to contact, and thus had no idea whether a personal injury claim, or even the tribunal proceedings, would be pursued.

☐ A gardener employed by a local authority direct service organisation (DSO) was given more work to do in less time. He complained about the increased workload but nothing was done and, ultimately, he went on sick leave suffering from insomnia, weepiness, tiredness and headaches. While still absent from work, although he continued to be paid (but not at full salary), he contacted a solicitor.

☐ A manager of a large company found his responsibilities diminished when first one and then a second manager were brought in from elsewhere. One of them became his superior and he was demoted. Over the next six months he was subjected to intimidatory treatment by the two outsiders, consisting, in part, of a series of humiliating disciplinary meetings. The subject of these meetings was his apparent failure to follow procedures related to expenses, but some of the allegations put to him were insubstantial and nit-picking, and the company seemed reluctant to accept his explanations. He was given an oral warning; no sooner had he successfully appealed against it than he was told the disciplinary process was to start all over again. On several occasions he complained of psychological harassment, and when ultimately he was given a highly critical appraisal report he resigned, unable to face any more of the treatment that had been meted out to him. He lost a stone in weight and developed irritable bowel syndrome, clinical depression and anxiety, and PTSD. He then took action against his former employer.

☐ A medically retired airline pilot claimed that the company he worked for operated an unsafe system of work, in that the pilots were required to fly about 15 'sectors' during the course of a normal shift (usually about eight hours). In addition they had to complete several mandatory pre-flight checks and logs in between each sector. He is of the opinion that, over the 17 years of his employment by the company, the failure to provide him with reasonable rest periods between sectors, and to ensure that he flew only a reasonable number of sectors in each shift, caused him stress that adversely affected his health. He therefore initiated a personal injury claim against his employer.

Reference

1 Under a conditional fee arrangement the client pays the solicitor's fees only if the outcome of the case is successful.

7   HANDLING WORKPLACE STRESS

Introduction

The aim of this chapter is to bring together earlier parts of the book and to discuss the ways in which workplace stress can be avoided, or at least minimised, by preventive action on the part of organisations and the individuals within them. Accepting that the prevention of all stress is an unreasonable ideal, however, this chapter also explores the various stress management interventions that can help employees to cope with the pressures of work and provide an outlet for their concerns, whether work-related or otherwise.

Attempts are made throughout the chapter to assess and comment on these measures in the light of potential legal liability. It concludes by illustrating in some detail the way in which employers can fairly dismiss those who, regardless of the reasonable efforts of the organisation to accommodate them, simply cannot cope with the demands of the job.

Employer options to deal with stress

In 1991 a survey carried out by the Confederation of British Industry (CBI) showed that, although 94 per cent of companies thought mental illness should be of concern to them, only about 10 per cent had any company programme to deal with it.[1] However, in recent years a growing interest in stress management and workplace health promotion has developed in the UK, particularly among organisations of US parentage. Now that stress litigation in the UK has become a reality, though not (as yet) to the extent experienced by the Workers' Compensation Scheme in the USA, that interest seems unlikely to diminish.

The actions that organisations can take are usually classified in one of two ways according to whether they target the organisation or the individual and where they stand on the following preventive/remedial scale:[2]

☐ primary intervention – concerned with taking preventive action to reduce or eliminate stressors (ie sources of stress) and with positively promoting a supportive and healthy work environment

☐ secondary intervention – concerned with the prompt detection and management of depression and anxicty by increasing self-awareness and improving stress-management skills

☐ tertiary intervention – concerned with the rehabilitation and recovery process of those individuals who have suffered or are suffering from ill health as a result of stress.

In general, secondary and tertiary interventions are aimed at the individual, whereas primary intervention targets the organisation or the organisation–individual interface. Although there has been considerable activity at the secondary and tertiary level, the perception is that primary strategies have so far been comparatively rare.[3] This was illustrated by a study carried out in the Manchester School of Management (UMIST) in 1994 in which 300 organisations were sent questionnaires asking them about their actions to reduce stress. Of the 50 companies that responded, only 12 per cent operated stressor-reduction strategies, whereas approximately 33 per cent made use of secondary interventions, and a similar number tertiary interventions. Interestingly, none at that time had introduced stress management with an eye to litigation, and just under half of those who had such programmes believed they were not doing enough to tackle the problem of stress.

Although treatment may be easier than cure, it may be a strategy that is effective only in the short term. Moreover, now that psychiatric harm has been equated with physical harm so far as employers' duties to their workforce are concerned, it seems likely that secondary and tertiary interventions will not of themselves be sufficient to satisfy the duty. Remedial action to 'cure' employees suffering from stress will be no more adequate in providing a safe system of working than would sitting back and allowing accidents to occur and then providing efficient on-site medical facilities to deal with them. How, then, are employers to proceed?

Moving forward – assessment of risk

It is self-evident that employers cannot take appropriate steps to make the workplace safe from psychiatric harm unless they know what, in their own organisation, the risks of harm are. Some form of risk assessment is therefore necessary not only as a positive requirement of the Management of Health and Safety at Work Regulations 1992 and other related legislation (see Chapter 5), but also as a precondition to taking the necessary steps to satisfy the duty of care. The starting point must therefore be for employers to acquaint themselves with literature such as the HSE guidelines (or Chapter 3 of this book!), which will inform them of the sources of stress and how stress manifests itself at the workplace. They will then be better placed to assess which issues are relevant for them; in fact, recent efforts have been made to specifically calculate the risk mathematically, using the Occupational Stress Indicator.[4]

Not all stressors exist, or exist to the same extent, within all occupations and industries. For example, the risk of personal assault is a significant occupational stressor among bus drivers in the UK transport industry,[5] whereas a major source of stress for income tax officers was found to be autocratic management style and lack of consultation.[6] Other research has found differences between institutions and organisations in the same industry or business sector, and even between different subcultures and status groups within the same organisation. Consequently, the type of action required by an organisation to reduce or eliminate workplace stressors varies according to the kinds of stressor, the level of coping skills of those involved, and the culture of the organisation.[7] In the examples given above, stress reduction might suggest a possible ergonomic solution in the case of bus drivers, whereas a change in management style towards greater employee participation is more likely to reduce the stress experienced by tax officers.

Before making arrangements for putting into practice the necessary preventive and protective measures, organisations need answers to questions such as the following:

- What levels of stress exist at present within the organisation?
- Is job satisfaction, and physical and psychological health, better in some areas than in others?
- How do our levels of stress compare with those of other occupational groups?
- Does it look as if we have a problem?
- If we do, can we identify its cause – what appear to be the stressors?
- Are the stressors departmental, site-specific or organisation-wide?

In order to find the answers, organisations may feel it helpful to be guided by a diagnosis of the problem from the viewpoint of the workforce by carrying out a stress audit. Stress audits typically take the form of a self-report questionnaire administered to employees on an organisation-wide, site or departmental basis. In addition to identifying the sources of stress at work and those employees most vulnerable to stress (not necessarily on an individual basis), the questionnaire may provide data about the levels of employee job satisfaction, coping behaviour, and physical and psychological health compared to those in similar occupational groups and industries. They can thus be an effective way of directing organisational resources into areas where they are most needed. Audits also provide a means of monitoring stress levels and employee health regularly over time, as well as a baseline from which subsequent interventions can be evaluated.

Diagnostic instruments such as the Occupational Stress Indicator[8] are increasingly being used by organisations for this purpose. They are usually administered through occupational health or personnel/human resource departments in consultation with a psychologist. In smaller companies, an alternative procedure is to hold employee discussion groups or develop checklists that can be administered on a more informal basis. The agenda for these discussions or checklists should address issues such as the following:

- job content and work-scheduling
- physical working conditions
- relationships at work

□ communication systems and reporting arrangements
□ employee expectations.

Another alternative is to ask employees to keep for a few weeks a stress diary in which they record any stressful events they encounter during the course of the working day. Pooling this information on a group or departmental basis can be useful in identifying universal and persistent sources of stress.

Two important comments need to be made at this point. The first is that if employers carry out risk assessments or stress audits that identify problems relating to a particular occupational group such as 'shift managers' (or occurring within a given department) and then do nothing to address the problems, they leave themselves vulnerable to legal claims from individuals within those groups or departments. Should one such individual suffer a stress-related illness, employers will find it more difficult to argue that the employee's injury was unforeseeable if they had, in effect, been previously 'put on notice'. On the other hand, employers who do nothing even to investigate the issue of stress in the workplace are also at risk, because they will be deemed to have the knowledge that would have been available to them had they acted reasonably in informing themselves.

The second point is that a key factor in tackling this problem is the development of the kind of organisational climate in which stress is recognised as a feature of modern industrial life and not interpreted as a sign of weakness or incompetence. It is therefore crucial that there is a demonstrable commitment to the issue of stress and mental health at work from senior management. The UMIST study referred to earlier found that such was not always the case, and that many organisations were unable to introduce stress management because they had not successfully gained senior management commitment towards initiatives. A group training manager interviewed for the study put it this way:

> But at the end of the day we need the Board's 'clout' to get the programmes there . . . I think the greatest resistance we will have will come from our most senior people, I have no doubt about that.

Some of the questionnaire respondents appeared extremely

negative about stress at work, or regarded it as entirely the problem of the individual concerned. One commented:

> In many respects I am very leery about this, I mean it's one of those current trendy areas, sort of 'Oh dear, people are under stress. Is it all getting a bit too much for you?'

These unenlightened views about the sort of experiences to which individuals such as those described in Chapter 6 were subjected are clearly a major stumbling-block to having workplace stress treated in a sensible and reasonable fashion. It is understandable that people in senior jobs who are themselves relatively tough and resilient find it hard to comprehend why subordinates have difficulty in coping. Nevertheless, only if top management take the issue on board and are prepared to scrutinise the very culture of the organisation to discover whether it inherently promotes stress amongst its employees (eg by expectations of long working hours) will anything positive be achieved.

Primary intervention: stressor reduction

This section explores a range of preventive measures that organisations may take, although it is in no way intended to be exhaustive. The whole point about carrying out a diagnosis of risks to mental well-being is that organisations should come up with a solution tailored to their own needs. The following are therefore simply the most commonly recognised, or most likely to be of wide application.

Recruitment

Recruiting with care

Although employers who simply screen out at the recruitment stage anyone with a past history of mental disorder are likely to contravene the provisions of the DDA (see Chapter 5), that is not to say that they cannot take care in recruiting to appoint someone who is capable of doing the job. That of course implies that there is a need to know what the job entails. However, there seems little evidence as yet that employers seek out particular personality types unless, for instance, the job is dangerous and someone safety-conscious is needed. If, in the future, they should begin to use pre-employment medicals and psychometric testing to identify, and avoid employing, susceptible individuals in inherently stressful jobs, they should be aware that most of the employees described in the case studies in Chapter 6 had no history of mental illness.

Two points should be noted in relation to enquiry about mental health prior to selection:

☐ It may be fair to dismiss employees who are subsequently found to have lied about the matter. In *O'Brien* v *Prudential Assurance Ltd*[9] the employee was specifically asked about mental health during a routine medical examination for the job of district agent, but failed to disclose that he had a long history of mental disorder. Subsequently this came to light and he was dismissed. The company had a policy of not employing persons with a background of mental illness as district agents, because the job entailed visiting people's homes. It was held that O'Brien's lack of honesty about a material mental health consideration constituted 'some other substantial reason' for dismissal within S98(1)(b) of the ERA.

☐ Employers who do ask for disclosure of medical records will thereby be put on notice of any mental illness the individual has suffered, and may find it hard to argue that a recurrence was not foreseeable.

Although the decision should perhaps be confined to the special circumstances of the case, there is legal authority to the effect that it may be a term of the contract that an employee is in good health, as measured by sickness absence. In *Leonard* v *Fergus and Haynes Civil Engineering Ltd*[10] the contract contained a term that any employee absent for two shifts in a period of a fortnight would be deemed unfit for work on a North Sea oil platform. Mr Leonard's dismissal for ill health was upheld on the basis of his inability to comply with a fundamental term of his contract.

Warning about the risks

Although recruiting only the mentally robust may be fraught with difficulty, both legally and in practice, a more feasible and generally applicable measure is that of warning recruits about the potential stresses they are likely to experience in a given job. These may be, for example:

- long working hours
- working under pressure or to deadlines
- travelling away from home and disruption to home life
- working alone
- heavy responsibilities, eg for large budgets.

Simply warning the employee of the risks is unlikely to be sufficient to fulfil the duty of care if some of the pressures could have been avoided, but it may go some way to showing that an employer who saw the inherent risks acted reasonably in the circumstances. In the case of *Gillespie* v *Commonwealth of Australia* (see page 57), the judge specifically found that the plaintiff should have been warned about the stressful conditions he was likely to meet when he was posted to Caracas, Venezuela.

Having warned or given sufficient information about the risks, however, it does seem that employers will not be liable simply by taking on an individual they believe may be susceptible to stress. In the case of *Withers* v *Perry Chain Co Ltd*[11] the plaintiff repeatedly contracted dermatitis because of a sensitivity to the grease with which her job brought her into contact. Having on each occasion apparently recovered, she thereafter presented herself for work as fit. The Court of Appeal ruled that the employer was not under a duty to refuse to employ, or to dismiss, an employee merely because there might be some slight risk (*sic*) to the employee in doing the work.

Preventive measures at the level of the organisation

Organisational culture

Different types of organisational culture nurture particular values, attitudes and styles of work to create psychologically different work environments. As noted earlier in this chapter, developing a culture that is supportive rather than confrontational, one that allows people to express their uncertainties without penalties, is essential in dealing with workplace stress. A culture in which 'office politics' is rife, or where employees lack control because they are not involved in decisions that affect them, or where managers and supervisors are unsupportive and insensitive to employees' problems, will not be one in which the issue of stress at work can be effectively tackled. Changing the culture may therefore involve increased participation by the workforce, more open communication, and more effective consultation with employees. Participation in decision-making also promotes higher job satisfaction, whereas a lack of it leads to negative outcomes such as depression, low self-esteem and absenteeism (see Chapter 3). At ICI-Zeneca a crucial step in beginning to handle workplace stress was the sending of a letter signed by the chief executive officer to all departmental heads acknowledging that the increased demands of the business had caused some problems, and in effect warning managers about the dangers of putting people under too much pressure.[12] The letter underlined the credibility of the problem of workplace stress and was seen as a vital precursor to putting subsequent practical proposals into effect.

Job factors

Chapter 3 highlighted a number of factors intrinsic to the job that employees find stressful, and scrutiny of various aspects of the job may lead to their being redesigned. Examples of the sort of options that can be considered are:

☐ job rotation
☐ job-sharing
☐ job enlargement
☐ flexible working
☐ development of more autonomous workgroups
☐ working from home
☐ short or evening shifts.

There is always the possibility, however, that jobs themselves may be difficult to redesign in a fundamental way because they are inherently stressful. They may, for example, involve violence or danger; continuous contact with, or responsibility for, people; or exposure to human suffering or injury. Nevertheless, jobs must be 'doable', with given levels of support, and there is no reason why employees should tolerate stressful working environments with unreasonable levels of noise, dust or dirt, or uncomfortable working temperatures. In fact, employers who do not tackle such issues will fail to satisfy the duty to provide a safe system of working and, as indicated in Chapter 5, employees who find the conditions intolerable may well succeed in unfair dismissal claims. Two further tribunal cases serve as a reminder:

□ *Piggot Bros* v *Jackson*.[13] Failure by the employer to get a definitive answer to the cause of symptoms produced by a certain material was a failure to take reasonable steps to deal with the problem. In the light of employees' fears for their own health, and until more was done and an answer emerged, or it had become clear that nothing further could be done, it was not reasonable to dismiss employees who refused to work with the material. (This would now come into the category of automatically unfair 'health and safety' dismissals.)

□ *Whitbread plc t/a Thresher* v *Gullyes*.[14] Mrs Gullyes was a branch manager put in charge of a branch that had both staff and operational problems; this was a post that more experienced staff had refused to accept. The job necessitated Mrs Gullyes's working 76 hours a week. She eventually resigned, having found that her two most experienced staff were removed while she was on holiday. It was held that she had been (unfairly) constructively dismissed: she had been placed in an untenable position because she had not been given sufficient staff hours to enable her to perform her contractual duties.

The latter case highlights the increasingly significant issue of working hours. The flexibility demanded by organisations in the 1990s, the longer opening times in the retail sector, and the Working Time Regulations 1998 all guarantee that the question of what is appropriate in terms of working hours is likely to remain on the agenda for the foreseeable future. Given that average working hours in the UK are the longest in Europe, and that evidence points to the fact that subjecting employees to excessive hours is not only stressful but detrimental both to work performance and family life, this is an aspect of working conditions that employers would do well to investigate.

Traditional notions of whether a job is 'safe' now also need to be re-examined from the point of view of security. Employers who fail to take reasonable steps to prevent raids, for example in banks and building societies, or to protect employees from violent attacks, not only put their employees at risk of high levels of stress but put themselves at risk of receiving legal claims should employees suffer injury, whether physical or arising out of trauma.

Preventive measures at the organisation/individual interface

Management style

The case studies in Chapter 6 make it clear that one of the most important questions for an organisation to address is whether its managers are fit to manage. Regardless of whether a risk assessment points to a 'relationship' problem within a given department, for example, it seems essential that managers and supervisors are given the appropriate training to enable them to deal effectively and sensitively with the 'people' issues with which they are involved.

Given the degree of harm that can be caused by persecution, or by bullying and aggressive styles of management, there can be no excuse for allowing such behaviour. Organisations would be wise to make it clear that bullying, whether by colleagues or superiors, is a disciplinary offence, and it can logically be included as part of a harassment policy. Employers must also ensure that disciplinary procedures and personnel policies such as performance-related pay and appraisal are operated fairly. Many employees find these inherently stressful (see pages 140–43) and, if operated unfairly, they can lead to intense frustration and discontent. Ideally, management style needs to be accessible without being interventionist, and managers should ensure both that their staff are informed about matters that affect them and also that, wherever possible, they are consulted about such issues. It is also important that employees are given proper management support, including support by senior management to those in junior and middle ranks. This is especially so if, for example, they are newly promoted or lacking in experience. In the *Whitbread* case above, an additional reason for the finding of constructive dismissal was that Mrs Gullyes's employer knew she lacked experience and needed back-up, but failed to provide it (see also the case of *Leech* v *CRS*, pages 74–5).

Clearly, it is desirable that those responsible for staff are well informed about sources of stress at work and able to recognise the symptoms of stress in their subordinates. These can include:

- unaccustomed gloominess
- irritability
- lack of concentration
- loss of motivation and commitment
- increase in sickness absence
- poor decision-making
- increase in wastage and error rates
- reduction in output or productivity
- deterioration in planning and control of work.

For further details, see for example the HSE guidelines.

However, simply to recognise the symptoms of stress will not be sufficient. Managers must also be prepared to deal sympathetically and sensitively with those whom they perceive to be suffering from stress. Moreover, their attitude must be conveyed to those for whom they are responsible, otherwise sufferers may be reluctant to admit to problems or deal with them constructively.

Management of change

The rapid pace of technological development and fierce competition in world markets has made change in organisations inevitable. Because hardly anyone at work will have escaped the effects of change, and because uncertainty of expectations is stressful, it is logical that change ought to be managed correctly. What is particularly important is that managers are trained to understand the implications of change, that they communicate with staff and, if possible, allow them to participate in decisions. Employers sometimes try to hide news of detrimental changes, such as impending redundancies, from their workforce in the misguided belief that this will avoid 'worrying them'. In reality, rumours and fears can cause more stress than knowing the facts.

From a legal standpoint, employers may be able to insist that employees adapt to new working methods without being in breach of contract (see, for example, *Cresswell* v *Board of Inland Revenue*[15]), although there will be corresponding obligations on the employer to provide retraining to cope with the change. Nevertheless, whether or not changes involve alterations to contractual terms and conditions, negotiation is always preferable to the enforcement of change, which is likely to lead to long-lasting and deep-seated resentment.

Individuals' roles in the organisation

So far as they are able, organisations should ensure that the right people are doing the right job – in other words, that there is a good job-worker fit. Given the stress that can be generated by job ambiguity and uncertainty, it may also be advisable to ensure clarity of job role by examining job descriptions to make sure that they adequately reflect the job as it is now expected to be done, or by drawing them up where such do not exist. It may be worthwhile noting that one of the complaints made by several managers who have taken legal advice about suing their employers was that they were tired of never knowing where they stood, and always 'having the goalposts moved'. It is also important that individuals have a sense of career development so that they do not stagnate and lose motivation.

Harassment and bullying policies

One of the most positive actions that can be taken to improve the working lives of large numbers of employees is to introduce policies that work effectively to reduce or eliminate harassment and bullying (see Appendix 5). Because harassment and bullying almost inevitably generate stress and, in some cases (as discussed in Chapters 5 and 6), lead to serious stress-related illnesses, it is welcome to note that many organisations are now regarding them as a serious management issue. The point to be made about effective policies that classify such behaviour as a serious disciplinary offence (and are actually put into practice) is that they not only provide a remedy for victims but may also make potential harassers or bullies think twice before indulging in such behaviour. In other words, they can have a deterrent effect.[16]

The diminishing number of employers who do nothing about harassment (in particular) because they say it 'isn't a problem in my workplace' are often deluding themselves. The reality is usually that those who are subjected to it perceive that nothing will be done and therefore do not complain.

Employment tribunals hearing discrimination claims based on sexual and racial harassment appear at last to be using their powers in order to make:

> a recommendation that the respondent take within a specified period action appearing to the tribunal to be practicable for the purpose of obviating or reducing the adverse effect on the complainant of any act of discrimination to which the complaint relates (section 65(1)(c) SDA 1975; section 56(1)(c) RRA 1976).

In *Campbell* v *Datum Engineering Co Ltd*,[17] a Birmingham tribunal recommended that the company introduce a formal procedure for dealing with racial harassment that also contained an informal procedure, whereby the manager in charge spoke to the person complained of and so nipped the problem in the bud. Similarly, in *Dalziel* v *Muircroft plc*,[18] a Newcastle-upon-Tyne tribunal recommended the employer take steps to contact the Advisory, Conciliation and Arbitration Service (ACAS) and the Equal Opportunities Commission (EOC):

> with a view to obtaining appropriate literature and advice concerning the setting-up of a policy to deal with matters of sexual discrimination . . . that there should be suitable training and advice given to employees as to how to deal with such situations if they arise and to management as to how to prevent such occurrences in the future.

Although tribunals cannot enforce their recommendations in the organisation concerned, the making of recommendations has wider significance, in that they give a more general pointer to employers as to the standards currently expected of them.

Grievance procedures

Just as the tribunal in the Campbell case above spoke of the need to 'nip the problem in the bud', it is clearly desirable that employee complaints other than those related to harassment or bullying have a channel of expression via a grievance procedure before they build up into irreconcilable personality clashes or deep-seated resentment. It should be noted that the EAT has now held (in the case of *W A Goold (Pearmark) Ltd* v *McConnell and another*[19]) that an employer's failure to provide employees with a proper method of dealing with work-related grievances was a breach of an implied term in their contracts. The employees concerned were thus entitled to resign and claim constructive dismissal.[20] In the EAT's view, the right to obtain redress where the employment environment led to employees' having difficulties due to their working conditions or problems arising from a breakdown in human relationships was a fundamental and obvious one. (NB: preventive measures may not always succeed, but at least if a concerted attempt has been made to avoid the sort of problems discussed, employers will be in a stronger position to argue that they acted 'reasonably in the circumstances' where reasonableness is an issue.)

Preventive measures at the level of the individual

Essentially, these are measures that aim directly to promote positive health behaviours in the workplace (ie health promotion activities). They may include:

- □ the introduction of regular medical checks and health-screening
- □ the design of 'healthy' canteen menus
- □ the provision of on-site fitness facilities and exercise classes
- □ corporate membership at concessionary rates of local health and fitness clubs
- □ the introduction of cardiovascular fitness programmes
- □ advice on alcohol and dietary control (particularly cutting down on high-fat food, salt and sugar)
- □ smoking-cessation programmes
- □ advice on lifestyle management.

For small organisations without the facilities of, for example, an occupational health department, there are external agencies that can provide a range of health-promotion programmes.

Secondary intervention: stress-management techniques

Stress-management techniques generally focus on educating employees about stress and its manifestations and on training them both on how to avoid stress and on how to manage it when it occurs. Some of the following activities are usually covered:

☐ relaxation
☐ biofeedback
☐ exercise and behavioural modification
☐ time management
☐ assertiveness training
☐ problem-solving skills
☐ lifestyle advice and planning.

Stress education and stress-management courses aim therefore to help individuals recognise the symptoms of stress in themselves and others, and to extend and develop their coping skills and abilities, and their stress resilience. Although stress management training is often offered only to employees in white-collar professions in order to combat so-called 'executive stress', it can in fact be beneficial to all levels of staff. It is particularly useful in training managers to recognise stress in their subordinates and to be aware of their own managerial style and its impact on those they manage.

In many organisations, stress-management training is not formally established in its own right, but is an integral part of health promotion or 'wellness programmes'. For example, IBM's 'Plan for Life' scheme places the emphasis on pre-empting problems through self-awareness; it covers all aspects of health, including lifestyle, alcohol, diet and stress.

Evidence as to the success of secondary interventions is generally confusing and imprecise, partly on account of the variety of content and the fact that they are often embedded in broader health promotion programmes. Some recent studies, which have evaluated the outcome of stress-management training, have found a modest improvement in self-reported symptoms and psychological indices of strain[21] but little or no change in job satisfaction, work stress or blood pressure. Participants in a company-wide programme, for example, reported improvements in health, in the short term (ie three months post-intervention), but little was known about its long-term effect.[22] Other research evidence supports this view that stress-management programmes are effective in reducing stress in the short term.[23] Although assessment of the cost and longer-term benefits still remains problematic, the following are well documented:

☐ The New York Telephone Company's wellness programme, designed to improve cardiovascular fitness, saved the organisation $2.7 million in absence and treatment costs in one year alone.[24]

☐ General Motors Corporation reported a 40 per cent decrease in lost time and a 60 per cent decrease in accident and sickness benefits as a result of its programme.

Tertiary interventions: counselling/employee assistance programmes

Tertiary interventions are in effect coping strategies designed to assist employees who are already suffering negative effects of stress. As indicated earlier in this chapter, on their own they are unlikely to satisfy the employer's duty of care, but they may assume a more significant role in dealing with workplace situations in which some stressors cannot be eliminated. They may also be cost-effective in terms of easing back to work someone who has had time off with mental problems, rather than having to retire him or her early on medical grounds and then recruit and train a successor.

Organisations deciding to provide access to confidential and professional counselling services for employees with workplace problems or ones of a more personal nature (eg drug abuse, personal crises, marital and family problems) have the choice of doing so either through in-house counsellors or by buying in the services of outside agencies in the form of employee assistance programmes (EAPs). EAPs may be more expensive than using an 'in-house' approach (they typically cost £25-30 per employee per year) but they generally have the advantage of a 24-hour service that employees can contact from the privacy of their own home. There may also be a perception by employees of their greater confidentiality, because the counsellors are not company employees.

Whichever approach is chosen, however, it is important to ensure that counsellors have received recognised training and have access to a suitable environment for conducting the activity in an ethical and confidential manner. In addition to counselling in the strict sense, they can also provide information about and/or referral to appropriate treatment and support services. Employers should note the following points about counselling and EAPs:

☐ Although EAPs are generally regarded as remedial interventions, there is a growing perception that prompt provision of counselling following traumatic events at work (such as bank hold-ups) acts as a preventive measure in relation to the development of PTSD.

☐ Because counselling is a confidential activity, the problems of a given individual will not be revealed to management. It would therefore not be foreseeable that that individual was particularly sensitive, nor would the employer be in breach of duty by failing to act accordingly. Anecdotal evidence does suggest, however, that in the case of in-house counselling it is possible to feed a generalised issue (say about a given department) back to management without naming names. Employers would thereby be put on notice and would be legally vulnerable if they failed to respond.

☐ Employees are more likely to be willing to see counsellors or participate in stress-management programmes when the organisational culture is one in which stress-related problems are taken seriously. Acceptance of the need to take advantage of such programmes may otherwise be perceived as a sign of weakness, which could have a negative effect on career progression.

There have been some dramatic reports attesting to the cost benefit of EAPs and health promotion activities, although they have not been without criticism – for example, that the studies lack control groups, fail to use objective multiple measures, and are of cross-sectional rather than longitudinal design. Nevertheless, the counselling programme introduced in the Post Office resulted in a fall in absenteeism in one year of approximately 60 per cent.[25] Pre- and post-counselling measures showed marked improvement in the mental health and self-esteem of participating employees, although neither job satisfaction nor organisational commitment were affected to any significant degree. Catherine Green, senior manager in charge of Midland Bank's EAP, has pointed out that stress counselling can also 'enhance an employer's image as a caring organisation, lift the pressure on managers who are not qualified to deal with staff problems and can improve productivity in the workplace'.[26] Midland Bank believes its 'Openline' has prevented at least one suicide.

It is important to bear in mind that certain issues need to be addressed prior to the introduction of any programme to control stress. These include:

☐ a clear understanding of why an initiative is being taken

☐ a recognition of the potential benefits to be gained (evaluation)

☐ an understanding of the attitudes of employees and management to stress management and stress control

☐ a clear definition of who is involved (both internally and externally).[27]

Dismissal

Ultimately, employers cannot be expected to employ indefinitely individuals who are incapable of carrying out their jobs. Indeed, if it becomes apparent to the employer that a given individual cannot cope with the stresses and strains of the job, it may be more prudent to opt for dismissal rather than let him or her run the risk of a stress-related illness (or allow an existing illness to get worse). In the Walker case the judge commented that:

> When Mr Walker returned from his first illness the Council had to decide whether it was prepared to go on employing him in spite of the fact that he had made it sufficiently clear that he must have effective additional help if he was to continue at Blyth Valley.

Of course, one of the problems in this area is that many employees who are struggling to cope will be unlikely to admit it. There are many who perceive that their career progression is unlikely to be enhanced by such 'whingeing' (even in a supportive organisational climate!); they may even fear for their jobs. Nevertheless, once employees have taken time off and a GP has diagnosed 'stress' or a stress-related illness, employers are entitled to be cautious and to take a dispassionate view. They are likely to ask themselves, 'If I keep this person on – or take them back before they are entirely fit – am I risking a repetition of their illness or, worse, a deterioration of their condition?' Unless employers are very sure of their invulnerability to personal injury claims they may choose in the circumstances to terminate the person's employment. However, the timing of such a decision may be crucial. Should matters have progressed too far, an individual may be headed for a breakdown whether he or she quits the job or not. If employers jump the gun and fail to investigate adequately, or cut procedural corners, then at the very least an unfair dismissal claim is likely to ensue.

In Chapter 5, the importance of investigating properly the medical condition, consulting with the employee and following a fair procedure was stressed. It was also pointed out that, if there were reasonable steps that could have been taken to alleviate the stressful conditions, an employer who failed to do so prior to taking a decision to dismiss would not be acting 'reasonably in the circumstances' (see also the provisions of the DDA discussed on pages 86–87). There will no doubt be some employers who will weigh up the facts that to dismiss at too early a stage may cost them anything up to £56,900 in unfair dismissal compensation (although compensation under the DDA is unlimited), whereas to leave matters too long, or to keep employees on the books when their health continues to deteriorate, may result in claims for damages in a personal injury action of three or four times that amount.

The case below provides a particularly powerful and illuminating example of an employer who, faced with the situation of an employee absent because of a stress-related illness, managed to avoid the potential pitfalls and dismiss fairly. It is described in some detail because, when dealing with such illnesses, the tone and content of the communications involved assumes a greater significance than in cases of physical ill health. Insensitive treatment can very easily make stress-related illnesses a great deal worse.

The case of Cross v Cumberland Building Society [28]

The applicant was employed by the society in 1979. She worked as a part-time cashier clerk at the Preston branch, and until

1992 her performance appeared to be satisfactory. However, at that time the Society introduced two new systems: an appraisal system and a 'pass-back' system. The essence of the pass-back system was that counter staff were required to identify in their dealings with customers potential leads for new Society business. They would then 'pass back' those customers to non-counter staff who would engage in what could be lengthy discussions and the giving of advice. Those customers who merely required short transactions could thus be dealt with more quickly.

The Society's appraisal system was to operate on an annual basis unless a particular member of staff failed to reach a satisfactory performance level, in which case there would be a further appraisal after six months. If a member of staff received a substandard appraisal on two occasions within a short time, he or she would receive an oral warning. Failure to improve at a further review would warrant a written warning.

In February 1993 Mrs Cross's appraisal showed that she 'occasionally fell short' of the requirements of the job. A further appraisal in September showed that she did meet the requirements. However, in April 1994 Mrs Cross's appraisal was similar to that of February 1993, and this was reported to the assistant general manager, Mr McGlasson. He interviewed Mrs Cross about her performance on 13 June 1994 in the presence of her branch manager, Mrs Thompson. Mrs Cross responded that she did not believe in the pass-back system and doubted its potential for new business. Mr McGlasson explained the system and its advantages to Mrs Cross and issued her with an oral warning. This was confirmed in writing the following day, with a copy of the Society's disciplinary procedure.

Following the meeting, Mrs Cross was offered training at her branch in the form of having someone sit with her to assist her in operating the system. On 1 November Mr McGlasson had a further meeting with Mrs Cross during which he gained the impression that she now had a better grasp and acceptance of the system. However, at a subsequent appraisal meeting on 16 November Mr McGlasson took the view that Mrs Cross had failed to achieve the necessary improvement required of her, and hence she was issued with a written warning. Shortly afterwards Mr McVitie, who was responsible for personnel matters, received a doctor's certificate dated 19 November signing Mrs Cross off for two weeks suffering from 'debility'. The following sequence of events then took place:

1 On 2 December Mrs Thompson wrote to Mr McGlasson recording that she had spoken with Mrs Cross. Mrs Cross had indicated that her sickness was due to stress caused by work and the disciplinary action against her.

2 Two further doctor's certificates were received, certifying that Mrs Cross should refrain from work for four weeks from 2 December and 29 December 1994 respectively; both cited grounds of 'debility'.

3 Meanwhile Mrs Thompson again spoke with Mrs Cross on the phone to find out how things were going. She also wrote to her on 12 December. In her letter she asked Mrs Cross to keep in touch and told her that two staff had resigned, so 'As you can tell we are rather short-staffed'.

4 Mr McGlasson was becoming concerned at Mrs Cross's absence in the light of the other resignations: the branch was some distance from the Society's normal operating area and so it was not feasible for other branches to help out. Mr McGlasson was also aware that morale at the branch was not particularly good, owing partly to two armed robberies that took place in December 1993 and April 1994. He therefore asked Mrs Thompson to obtain Mrs Cross's permission to approach her GP and seek his opinion as to when Mrs Cross might return to work.

5 Mrs Thompson contacted Mrs Cross on 19 December to obtain her consent. Mrs Thompson wrote that:

> You have confirmed that in addition to prescribing anti-depressants, your doctor has recommended that you rest as much as possible. Obviously we are concerned for your sake that having been off for 5 weeks, the problems do not yet seem to have been resolved. However, I am sure that by following your doctor's advice and recommendations over the next few weeks, you will be able to make a speedy recovery and . . . return to work as soon as possible...I sincerely hope that your situation does improve in the near future and obviously would be grateful if you could continue to keep in touch on a regular basis.

6 Mrs Cross gave her consent and, on 4 January 1995, Mrs Thompson wrote to Mrs Cross's GP. She asked:

☐ When do you envisage that Mrs Cross will be fit to return to work?

☐ How does her present condition affect her ability to carry out her job?

☐ How will this condition affect her performance in future?

7 On 12 January Mrs Cross's GP replied, but so far as the Society was concerned the reply was inconclusive. He stated:

> I am unable to give you a firm date when I feel she will be fit to return to work but I am of the opinion that this is likely to be a lengthy illness...I do not envisage an early return to work.

8 This reply caused Mr McGlasson concern about making a decision regarding Mrs Cross's future and the problem of covering for her absence. Having received another certificate dated 28 January signing Mrs Cross off for four weeks, he met with Mr Dodd, another assistant general manager, to discuss the case. It was agreed to attempt to obtain a second medical opinion, and Mrs Cross was written to by Mr McVitie on 13 February to obtain her consent. Mr McVitie informed her that, if she refused, 'a decision about your continued employment will be taken on the basis of the current information available'. He also asked her to keep in touch with Mrs Thompson and he expressed the hope that:

> your situation improves in the near future and that you will be able to return to work once your present medical certificate runs out.

9 Mrs Cross did not, however, consent to another medical examination. She wrote: 'I do not feel due to my nerves and stressful state that I could cope with any more stress.' She said that she was satisfied to go along with her doctor's verdict. In consequence Mr McVitie wrote to Mrs Cross on 23 February saying that a decision would be made about her future with the Society on the basis of the information it had, and that this would be done on 8 March. He told her that her doctor's report and the impact of her absence

would be taken into account, and she was asked to recon-sider her decision about consent.

10 Mr McVitie prepared an internal memorandum on Mrs Cross for consideration by the Society's chief executive, by Mr Dodd and by Mr McGlasson. In it he recommended that she be written to on 15 March stating an intention to dis-miss her with effect from 31 March. The meeting of senior management took place on 6 March and it was decided that, in the absence of any indication of when Mrs Cross might return, and given the difficulties of covering her absence, the Society could not reasonably be expected to wait any longer.

11 Mr McGlasson wrote to Mrs Cross in those terms and advised her of her right of appeal.

The tribunal unanimously concluded that Mrs Cross's dis-missal was fair. They were impressed by the efforts the Society had made to communicate regularly with Mrs Cross and by the tone of the letters they wrote to her. The tribunal was aware that such communications might have been stressful for Mrs Cross but felt that in the circumstances there was little the Society could have done to avoid that happening. Mrs Cross had been kept fully in the picture and knew that the time had come when a decision had to be made. It was specifically found that the Society was not failing to act reasonably simply because Mrs Cross's entitlement to sick pay had still to expire; nor was it suggested that the appraisal scheme had been operated unfairly or oppressively. Although it was clearly difficult for employees like Mrs Cross to cope with change, they are expected to do so as long as employers provide appropriate training.

The tribunal felt that, in an ideal world, a personal visit could have been made to Mrs Cross to tell her that unless she con-sented to a second opinion the chances were that she would lose her job. Nevertheless they appreciated, first, that personal visits might themselves have been stressful and, secondly, that the Society had only to act 'reasonably in the circumstances' and not as models of perfection.

References

1 Buckingham L. 'A headache that just won't go'. The *Guardian*. 31 October 1992.

2 Cartwright S. and Cooper C. L. *Managing Workplace Stress*. London, Sage, 1997; Sutherland V. and Cooper C. L. *Strategic Stress Management*. London, Macmillan, 2000.

3 Murphy L. R. 'Occupational stress management: a review and appraisal'. *Journal of Occupational Psychology*. 57, pp1–5. 1984.

4 Clarke S. and Cooper C. L. 'The risk management of occupational stress'. *Health, Risk & Society*. 2 (2). 2000.

5 Dully C. A. and McGoldrick A. 'Stress and the bus driver in the UK transport industry'. *Work and Stress*. 4(1), pp17–27. 1990.

6 Cooper C. L. and Roden J. 'Mental health and satisfaction amongst tax officers'. *Social Science and Medicine*. 21(7), pp474–5. 1985.

7 See note 2.

8 Occupational Stress Indicator: The management set. Windsor, NFER-Nelson, 1988.

9 [1979] IRLR 140.

10 [1979] IRLR 235.

11 [1961] 3 All ER 676.

12 Teasdale E. and McKeown S. 'Managing stress at work: the ICI-Zeneca Pharmaceuticals Experience 1986-1993', in C. L. Cooper and S. Williams (eds), *Creating Healthy Work Organizations*, Chichester, John Wiley & Sons, 1994.

13 [1991] IRLR 309.

14 [1994] IRLIB 509.

15 [1984] IRLR 191.

16 Note also the relevance of such policies in establishing employer defences under discrimination legislation – see Chapter 5.

17 Case No 43749/94.

18 Case No 23842/94.

19 [1995] IRLR 516.

20 Had they lacked the necessary qualifying period of service

required to bring a case of unfair dismissal, they would nevertheless have been entitled to make an employment tribunal claim for breach of contract (section 3 Industrial Tribunals Act 1996).

21 Reynolds S., Taylor E. and Shapiro D. A. 'Session impact in stress management training'. *Journal of Occupational and Organisational Psychology*. 66, pp79–113. 1993.

22 Teasdale E. 'Stress management within the pharmaceutical industry', in C L. Cooper *et al*, *Stress Prevention in the Workplace*. Dublin. European Foundation for the Improvement of Living and Working Conditions, pp49–70, 1996. (See also Kompier M. and Cooper C. L., *Preventing Stress, Improving Productivity*, London, Routledge, 1999.)

23 Ivancevich J. M., Matteson M. T., Freedman S. M. and Phillips J. S. 'Worksite stress management interventions'. *American Psychologist*. 45, pp252–61. 1990.

24 Cooper C. L. 'The road to health in American firms'. New Society. pp335–6. 1985.

25 Allinson T., Cooper C. L. and Reynolds P. 'Stress counselling in the workplace – the Post Office experience'. *The Psychologist*. pp384–8, 1989.

26 Buckingham L. 'A headache that just won't go'. *The Guardian*. 31 October 1992.

27 Sutherland V. J. 'Managing stress at the workplace', in P. Bennett, J. Weinemann and P. Spurgeon (eds), *Current Developments in Health Psychology*, UK, Harwood Academic, 1990.

28 Case No 29131/95.

8 PRACTICAL CONSIDERATIONS AND FUTURE DEVELOPMENT

Introduction

Thus far this book has explored the legal principles and statutory provisions relevant to workplace stress. It has also discussed how employers can attempt to avoid the risks of legal liability and consequential financial penalties that can result when employees fall victim to stress-related illnesses. The final chapter now considers a variety of practical points related to legal actions and their success or failure, and the levels of damages likely to be involved in personal injury claims. The discussion is in no way intended to form a comprehensive explanation of the issues but merely to highlight aspects relevant to stress claims.

Although it draws attention to the difficulties confronting employees who want to bring claims, it would be very short-sighted of employers to ignore the possibility that others will follow in the footsteps of Mr Walker and win substantial damages for injuries caused by stressful working environments.

The book concludes by looking to the development of this branch of the law in the light of the opinions of personal injury solicitors.

Making a personal injury claim

The vulnerable plaintiff

From a plaintiff's point of view, making a personal injury claim is a protracted business. Whether those suffering from a stress-related illness that, they believe, is attributable to their working environment contact a solicitor directly or whether they make a claim through their union, at some point they will have to discuss the problem with their lawyer. Even this is likely to be stressful for them. It should not be forgotten that many such individuals will be vulnerable people who are suffering from depressive illnesses and will find that the legal process itself contributes to their stress. For this reason some potential plaintiffs may never even make it to the door of a solicitor.

Solicitors themselves are only too aware of such problems and realise that many cases will not reach court. They appreciate that certain individuals simply cannot face talking about their experiences; some have likened the difficulties to those present in rape cases and one solicitor noted that clients broke down in tears in around half of the initial interviews. It is inevitable that one of the factors to be weighed in the decision to pursue a claim is an assessment of the plaintiff as a witness in court.

Where employees allege bullying, persecution or victimisation as the trigger for their breakdown in health, solicitors also realise that supportive evidence may be hard to come by. There is an understandable reluctance on the part of potential witnesses who have remained in the defendant's employ to becoming embroiled in any contentious matter that might leave them open to criticism from other work colleagues or, more seriously, undermine their own position in the company. Some may experience the 'survival syndrome' – because they themselves managed to withstand the pressure, they cannot understand why others cannot do the same. In extreme cases they may even put the blame firmly on the shoulders of the plaintiff, attributing the injury to his or her own highly obsessive nature. Such cases may therefore hinge crucially on the credibility of the plaintiff's evidence.

Solicitors know too that defendants will, quite understandably, point to sources of stress from employees' domestic or personal backgrounds as proof that their condition is not attributable to the workplace. Employees who bring cases must therefore be able to withstand not only the strain of giving evidence but also that of being cross-examined on the issue of causation; they must be able to open up their personal lives to public scrutiny. Strong medical evidence tying the injury to the conditions of work will thus be crucial.

Medical evidence

No personal injury case, especially one involving alleged psychiatric injury, proceeds to court without the plaintiff's having been examined by at least one medical expert. In the normal course of events the expert in a stress-related case is a consultant psychiatrist, although sometimes the opinion of a psychologist is also sought. As explained in Chapter 4, diagnosis of a recognised psychiatric injury or mental disorder is needed before a legal case is viable; however, this is not always a simple matter. From a medical point of view there are difficulties in precise classification because disorders overlap and because individuals react in complicated and varying ways to the stressors imposed on them. At a practical level, however, the need for plaintiffs to be able to point to an identifiable psychiatric injury that they had suffered was not regarded by solicitors in general as a difficult hurdle to surmount.

Apart from the actual diagnosis of a psychiatric injury, the importance of the medical evidence lies in establishing the causal link between the allegedly stressful environment and the plaintiff's mental ill health. The psychiatrist's report normally attempts to assess the plaintiff's personality, whether any abnormalities or factors predisposing him or her to psychiatric illness exist, and how the stressful conditions have combined to produce the breakdown in health. Thus, in the Walker case, Professor Sims (Mr Walker's medical expert) gave evidence that Mr Walker was of 'normal' personality, lacking any underlying insecurity or undue sensitivity to the views or criticisms of others. In contrast, Dr Wood (the defendant's medical expert) testified that Mr Walker was 'towards the rigid end of the personality scale . . . extremely conscientious, but lacked flexibility'.

In the event, the judge regarded the medical experts' difference of opinion as unimportant because both of them accepted that Mr Walker had been made ill by the impact of his work on his personality. Where an initial medical examination cannot be so positive, because it reveals other problems in the employee's personal or domestic life, there appears to be a reluctance on the part of solicitors to pursue the claim, especially because they regard themselves as operating at the frontiers of legal development. They are understandably concerned about going to court or recommending union backing for what they regard as a 'dodgy' case. Moreover, there appears to be an equal hesitation about proceeding if the medical evidence suggests an underlying susceptibility to mental illness or that the stress has aggravated an existing complaint. In this case it is not because solicitors fear an inability to establish causation. Rather, unless the employer can be proved to have had knowledge, actual or 'constructive' (ie he either did or should have known of the employee's susceptibility), foreseeability of psychiatric illness will be more difficult to demonstrate.

Limitation

Personal injury cases

As in the case of personal injury actions based on physical harm, plaintiffs must bring their cases within a specified period, otherwise they will find themselves time-barred. The basic rule now contained in the Limitation Act 1980 is that personal injury actions must be brought within three years; this period begins when the damage is suffered. However, principally to accommodate victims of industrial diseases such as pneumoconiosis, who might be unaware for a considerable time that they had in fact contracted the disease, this strict rule has been ameliorated. Section 11 of the 1980 Act provides that an action can be brought within three years of the plaintiff's knowledge of the damage as an alternative to the date of damage itself.

As to the question of what is meant by the word 'knowledge', section 14 provides that time starts to run from the date upon which the plaintiff had knowledge of the following facts:

☐ that the injury in question was significant
☐ that the injury was attributable in whole or in part to the act or omission that is alleged to constitute negligence, ie that

the plaintiff knew the wrongful act was in fact the cause of the injury (or had contributed to it)
□ the identity of the defendant
□ if it is alleged that the act or omission was that of a person other than the defendant, the identity of that person and the additional facts supporting the bringing of an action against the defendant.

It is specifically provided (in section 14(2)) that any injury is significant if the person whose date of knowledge is in question would reasonably have considered it sufficiently serious to justify instituting proceedings for damages against a defendant who did not dispute liability and was able to satisfy a judgment. In the context of claims arising out of workplace stress, the possibility of time running only from the date of knowledge may be important, because unless the employee suffers something like a sudden heart attack it may be impossible to ascertain at what point in time a number of symptoms of stress evolved into a medically diagnosable condition. In other words the date of damage may be uncertain.

However, it is not merely a plaintiff's actual knowledge that is relevant but (by virtue of section 14(3)) the knowledge that he or she might have been expected to acquire from facts:

□   observable or ascertainable by the plaintiff
□ ascertainable by the plaintiff with the help of medical or other appropriate expert advice that it is reasonable for him or her to seek.

To take an example, suppose that Mr X begins to suffer the symptoms of irritable bowel syndrome. He has no idea what is wrong with him, or whether it could have been caused by the abusive behaviour of his line manager. He visits his GP who cannot make a firm diagnosis. Three months later, when the symptoms have become more marked, Mr X returns to his GP who tells him he believes him to be suffering from irritable bowel syndrome. At that point (at the latest), the employee has suffered the damage and, were it not for section 11 of the Act, time would start to run against him. The effect of section 11 is therefore that time would begin to run only from the point when:

□ he reasonably could have known, or actually knew, that his
  condition had been caused by his bullying line manager
□ such a condition was sufficiently serious to justify his suing
  his employer.

Much would therefore depend upon whether the GP linked Mr
X's condition to his working environment or whether the causal
link were to be established in some other way.

An important point to make is that 'knowledge' does not
include 'knowledge that a cause of action existed'. In other
words, if Mr X knew (or should have known) that he had suffered an injury caused by the workplace, it would be irrelevant
that he did not know he could sue his employer in such circumstances (or that he delayed in bringing proceedings for personal reasons, such as fear of losing his job). This is particularly
significant in the context of work-related psychological harm,
because prior to the *Walker* case employees who were bullied or
overworked may have had no idea that they could have sought
redress if their health was affected. As the case of Mr E illus-
trates (see Chapter 6, pages 102–105), it is likely that many
employees who simply left their jobs or took early retirement in
the 1970s and 1980s may have felt that they should be able to
bring claims against their employers, yet will be barred because
they are out of time. Courts do have a discretion to extend the
time period in appropriate cases, but such factors as the length
of the delay and the possible prejudice to the defendant would
then become important, as well as the reason for the delay.
According to solicitors, however, many judges take the view that
proceedings should be issued sooner rather than later, even if
not all the evidence needed to prove whether the injury is work-
related is yet available. They are unsympathetic to extensions
on such grounds.

Limitation in tribunal cases

If employees decide to make applications to employment tribunals as well as, or instead of, personal injury claims, they
must act with rather more speed, because time limits in these
tribunals work in months rather than years. In such claims the
main cause of action is typically a dismissal or an act of discrimination, and the 'injury' is in that sense only an incident to

the claim. Nevertheless, as explained in Chapter 5, it may well be reflected in the compensation awarded.

The employment tribunal 'rules' are that in cases of:

☐ unfair dismissal (including constructive dismissal)

   ☐ Application is to be made within three months of the effective date of termination (if notice is given, the effective date of termination is the date the notice expires).

   ☐ Claims out of time will fail unless the tribunal finds it was not 'reasonably practicable' to bring the claim in time. This is a fairly strict test, but conceivably an employee who left his or her job suffering from a mental disorder might be in such a state that it was indeed not reasonably practicable to initiate proceedings until some sort of recovery had taken place.

☐ race/sex/disability discrimination

   ☐ Application is to be made within three months of the act complained of.

   ☐ An act extending over a period shall be treated as done at the end of that period. This provision can be especially pertinent to cases of prolonged harassment or victimisation, in which, rather than treating each incident as an isolated act of discrimination (which can often render the earlier acts out of time) the behaviour is seen as a single act of discrimination extending over a period of time. Such an interpretation of the harassment is important from the point of view of compensation because if, for example, only the last act of harassment took place within the three-month period, damages for injury to feelings would be considerably less.

   ☐ Tribunals can nevertheless hear claims out of time if, in all the circumstances, it is just and equitable to do so.

Damages in personal injury cases

In Chapter 5 an indication was given of the levels of compensation awarded by employment tribunals. We now discuss briefly the principles that guide awards of damages in the civil courts, and their division into two categories – namely, 'general' and 'special' damages.

Damages in personal injury cases are generally assessed at trial on a once-and-for-all basis, and any likely future deterioration must be built into the award. Thus, for example, damages can be awarded for risk of relapse, and this may be important in stress cases because psychiatric injury can leave the sufferer vulnerable in the future. A medical report in respect of one of the case-study individuals (in Chapter 6) noted that '[he] will remain for his lifetime at a permanently higher risk of psychological disorder should he experience trauma'.

There is, however, one notable exception to the once-and-for-all rule. The Supreme Court Act 1981 (section 32A, inserted by the Administration of Justice Act 1982) gives the court power to assess damages in two stages if:

> there is proved or admitted to be a chance that at some definite or indefinite time in the future the injured person will, as a result of the act or omission which gave rise to the course of action, develop some serious disease or suffer some serious deterioration in his physical or mental condition.

This provision could be useful in the case of an employee who, for instance, had experienced a traumatic event at work, because the evidence might well establish that he or she could suffer a breakdown many years later.

General damages

General damages reflect non-pecuniary losses and are awarded for pain, suffering and loss of amenities of life. When considering pain and suffering, it must be remembered that, in the context of workplace stress claims, the victims may have suffered not only psychiatric illness but also stress-induced physical illnesses such as ulcers, heart attacks, hypertension and diabetes. 'Pain and suffering' can also include the suffering caused by the knowledge that their expectation of life has been shortened, as may be the case when the employee has had a heart attack, for example.

Nevertheless, in awards for psychiatric injury it is likely that 'loss of amenities of life' will also be a significant feature, because such injuries tend to affect all aspects of a person's life. It has been held to include:

□ sexual dysfunction
□ loss of marriage prospects
□ loss of enjoyment of family life
□ loss of enjoyment of work
□ injuries to the senses.

When one considers that symptoms of depressive disorders are typically a loss of interest or pleasure (or both) in normal activities, insomnia and diminished appetite, and that anxiety disorders may lead to feelings of unreality and fear of dying, it is not difficult to appreciate the relevance of loss of amenities of life to stress-related claims. Many sufferers experience extreme fatigue not only as a symptom of depression but also because their sleep is itself disturbed, and this detrimentally affects not only them but also relationships within the family. Some individuals begin to drink more heavily, sexual appetite may be reduced, and they feel hopelessness and low self-esteem; in short, their quality of life is reduced.

In the typical personal injury case based on physical harm, an aggregate sum is awarded for pain, suffering and loss of amenity; guidelines have evolved that suggest a bracket within which it is appropriate to select a figure for a given injury, such as the loss of an eye or paraplegia. Decided cases of psychiatric injury are, for the most part, fairly recent and are typically for 'nervous shock', or else they arise as a consequence of a physical injury. They are also more difficult to classify than physical injuries. Nevertheless, they have now occurred with such frequency that scales of compensation for different levels of psychiatric damage are included in the 1994 Judicial Studies Board Guidelines[1] as follows:

□ severe damage – £22,500 to £45,000
□ moderately severe damage – £8,500 to £20,000
□ moderate damage – £2,500 to £7,500
□ minor damage – £500 to £1,500.

In the case discussed earlier under the 'egg-shell skull' rule (see page 46) of Mrs Brice, whose mental state was so severely affected that on three occasions she was admitted to hospital under the Mental Health Act 1983, general damages were assessed at £22,500. Given that the case was decided in 1984 she would clearly have fallen within the 'severe damage' bracket on today's figures. Likewise, in 1993 the fireman Mr Hale who suffered PTSD following his involvement in the King's Cross Underground fire (see page 50) received £27,500. Although his condition was described as one of 'moderate severity', his career in the fire service was effectively over, and the judge commented that:

> He will continue to suffer from a deep-rooted depression which is unlikely to abate, and affects his whole outlook on life.[2]

Special damages

Special damages reflect losses that are financially quantifiable, however imprecisely. Although they can cover a range of heads of financial loss, including private medical treatment, it is loss of earnings and loss of earning capacity that are likely to be the most significant figures, far outweighing the sum of general damages for the injury itself.[3] Mr Walker (see Chapter 4) will never be a social worker again, and the other case studies in Chapter 6 demonstrate that, for many employees, a breakdown in their psychiatric health can effectively end their career. In many instances, not only is the employee's recovery likely to be slow and uncertain, but their increased vulnerability makes it improbable that he or she will be able to return to the sort of demanding jobs that he or she once performed. This will be reflected by the court's estimating the employee's future employment prospects, future incapacity and the number of working years of which he or she has been deprived.

Reductions to damages

In some circumstances the figure that would otherwise be awarded to a plaintiff is reduced. In the context of stress-related cases, the following are the most common situations in which this occurs:

- ☐ The plaintiff is found to be already suffering from a psychiatric disorder, which was worsened by the effects of the workplace stress – although apportioning the damages may be extremely difficult.
- ☐ The plaintiff is found to have a predisposition towards such an illness. The damages might then be reduced to reflect the

chance that the illness might have developed in any case –
contrast 'the egg-shell skull rule', according to which a person
has a predisposition, but there is no evidence that the illness
would have occurred in the absence of the injury (see page
46). (As already indicated, solicitors are at present wary of
taking on cases in either of these last two circumstances.)

☐ Failure to mitigate – plaintiffs must take reasonable steps to
mitigate their loss, and therefore damages may be reduced if
the plaintiff unreasonably refuses to undergo the
recommended medical treatment. However, the position is
complicated in the case of psychiatric illness, because an
unwillingness to undergo treatment, or to talk about the
unpleasant events that caused the illness, may be part and
parcel of the illness itself. In cases of PTSD in particular, as
noted earlier, victims seek to avoid anything that reminds
them of the trauma, and may find recounting the incident
extremely distressing.

☐ Social security benefits – the extent to which various benefits
must be deducted from damages is a complex and uncertain
area, but it would seem that:

☐ benefits payable by reason of disability and inability to
work for five years from the onset of the injury are
deducted

☐ *ex gratia* payments by employers are not generally deducted

☐ proceeds of personal insurance policies are not deducted

☐ an occupational disability pension is not deducted

☐ contractual or statutory sick pay is deducted.

☐ 'Compensation neurosis' – it is sometimes suggested (even in
medical reports) that a plaintiff's condition is likely to
improve once the case is settled or, conversely, that the condition is not likely to improve until it has. However, particularly in the context of psychiatric harm, this is not
necessarily an oblique accusation of malingering, because in
many cases the legal process is itself stressful and can even
exacerbate the injuries. Victims may be above all conscious
that, ultimately, they will have to testify in court, and are
thus unlikely to recover until that hurdle is cleared.

Future developments

Until case law establishes more principles in this area it is difficult to predict how cases based on workplace stress will progress through the courts. Solicitors know that many cases will fizzle out because the medical evidence is not sufficiently strong, because witnesses will not come forward to support the plaintiff's case, or simply because at the end of the day the plaintiff feels unequal to the strain of giving evidence in the witness box. Some have expressed concern that vicarious liability may be an issue if the employee has been the victim of a workplace bully; others see problems in establishing foreseeability if the employee is the only one of a similarly placed group of workers who 'cracks'. Most cases at the present time will be brought by the unions, and solicitors know that unless they can say there is a more than an even chance of winning, the union will not fund the case.

Despite this, there is a strong consensus of opinion that Mr Walker will not be the last to bring a successful personal injury case based on stress at work. John Usher, Mr Walker's own solicitor, commented that, considering the deterioration in conditions for many employees since the time of Mr Walker's breakdown, there must be hundreds of potential 'John Walkers' equally damaged by their working environment. In early 1995, a London solicitor reported that he saw on average two to three middle managers a week who had given up the unequal struggle to cope. It is also clear that employers have had to settle cases, and one can confidently predict that for every such settlement reported by the media there were at least an equal number that, by reason of a confidentiality clause, do not reach the ears of the general public.

The evidence that stress at work is on the increase seems incontrovertible. According to data assembled by the (then) IPD in 1998, a 1996 survey by the European Foundation for the Improvement of Living and working Conditions found that 28 per cent of European workers believe their health is affected by stress at work. A 1997 survey by a long-term disability insurer found claims for compensation arising from mental problems had increased by 90 per cent over the previous five years. The Health and Safety Executive (HSE) estimates that 60 per cent of all work absence – 40 million working days per year – is caused by stress-related illnesses. Furthermore, again according to the HSE, one in five employees admit to taking time off work because of work-related stress (while one in 13 have consulted their GP on stress-related problems). Finally, in a 1999 survey the CBI claimed that stress costs the UK some £10 billion per year.

In the light of all this powerful evidence, it is hardly surprising that the message about increased stress at work, and with it the potential for claims, is now being heard far more widely. *The Sunday Times* reported in 1994 that middle-class professionals such as dentists, teachers and nurses had seen a sharp rise in companies' premiums for permanent health insurance as insurers covered themselves for the substantial rise in insurance claims from stress-related illnesses.[4] Many solicitors liken workplace stress to RSI and see litigation growing if, like RSI, stress claims become 'popular'. Others take the view that people who in the past would simply have resigned and taken another job, or whose plight has been masked by the ability to take early retirement on medical grounds, are now being alerted to the fact that they do not simply have to put up with ill-treatment or get out, and are prepared to do something more positive to stop it.

If, therefore, stress litigation is set to rise, what reaction can be expected from employers' liability insurance companies? The perception of some solicitors is that stress claims are more likely to be defended vigorously, because insurance companies believe that such litigation will cost them considerable sums unless they take a tough stance from the start. It also seems likely that they will ask employers what they are doing about the issue of stress at work. As Duncan Campbell, assistant liability manager at the UK's largest employers' liability insurers, Eagle Star, said in 1994 shortly after the Walker judgment:

> As insurers we would look at the insured's approach to health and safety generally. Stress has not been a big issue until now, but clearly it is going to have a serious effect in the future.[5]

Unless employers take action there seems little doubt that workplace stress will be the focus of continued litigation. The HSE guidelines, the publicity arising from the Walker case, pressure from insurance companies, the willingness of unions to regard stress-related illness as an industrial disease, and the propensity for unions such as the GMB, MSF, and UNISON to take up bullying at work as a health and safety issue must alert all employers to the fact that this is a problem to be faced. If they do not, it will cost them – in increased premiums, in excesses where claims are successfully made, and in the damage suffered throughout the organisation in terms of poor morale and sickness absence.

Of course, the mere existence of legal claims will not in itself be significant if they do not succeed; judicial attitudes will therefore be equally important in shaping the progress of the law in this area. Although judges have traditionally been reluctant to find in favour of plaintiffs claiming 'nervous shock' for fear of opening the floodgates of litigation, developments in other branches of criminal and civil law point to an increasing recognition by the courts of psychiatric injury as genuine and nontrivial. In the case of *R. v Chan Fook*,[6] for example, the appellant was charged with assault occasioning 'actual bodily harm' contrary to section 47 of the Offences Against the Person Act 1861. The Court of Appeal held that where there was evidence that an assault had caused some psychiatric injury, the jury should be directed that the injury was capable of amounting to actual bodily harm. In the course of their judgment the court referred to the speech of Lord Wilberforce in the earlier case of *McLoughlin v O'Brien*,[7] in which he said that:

> Whatever is unknown about the mind-body relationship . . . it is now accepted by human science that recognisable and severe physical damage to the human body and system may be caused by the impact, through the senses, of external events on the mind.

On the civil side also, the Court of Appeal has demonstrated an awareness of the need to protect against psychiatric harm in the context of harassment (*Khorasandjian v Bush*[8]). Although the legal basis of the decision was not entirely clear, the court granted an injunction to restrain the defendant from persistently telephoning a woman who had ended their previous friendship. The court commented that:

> Although it could not be said, as yet, that she was suffering from any physical or psychiatric illness . . . the cumulative effect of continued and unrestrained further harassment such as she had undergone would cause such an illness.

The court thus recognised the seriousness of the victim's situation and the enormous weight of stress under which she had been placed. Subsequent to the case, the Protection from Harassment Act 1997 was passed, specifically providing for the award of damages for any anxiety caused by unlawful harassment.[9]

No doubt many strong cases based on stress-related harm will continue to be settled and will not form part of developing case law, but it seems inevitable that from time to time there will be one that will fight. The future of this litigation must therefore depend to a great extent on employers and the decisions they make about whether, and how seriously, to take the question of stress at work. Whereas no one can take all the stress out of working life, any more than they can make any other part of our lives stress-free, employers can come to regard this issue as a health and safety issue and do what is reasonable to mitigate its effects. The result will be not only to shield them from costly and time-consuming litigation but should also pay dividends in terms of reduced absenteeism, improved morale and better working relationships. Otherwise we may find, to paraphrase Mr Walker's solicitor, that:

> The John Walker case beat the first path through the jungle. It will become progressively easier until the path becomes a highway.[10]

References

1 Judicial Studies Board. *Guidelines for Assessment of General Damages in Personal Injury Cases*. 2nd edn. London, Blackstone Press, 1994.

2 The *Guardian*. 'King's Cross fireman awarded £147,000'. 5 November 1993.

3 See note 2. The sum for general damages represented only £27,500 in the total sum of £147,000.

4 Drake L. 'Professionals pay more to guard against stress'. *The Sunday Times*. 27 November 1994.

5 Campbell D. 'Shock awards put insurers under stress'. *Insurance Weekly*. 24 November 1994.

6 [1994] 2 All ER 552.

7 [1982] 2 All ER 298.
8 [1993] 3 All ER 669.
9 The Act makes it a criminal offence to pursue a course of conduct amounting to harassment and also makes it possible to obtain an injunction and damages if a civil claim is pursued. Although its provisions were targeted principally at 'stalking' behaviour, there is no reason why the Act could not be applied in a workplace context.
10 In conversation with the authors, October 1995.

APPENDIX 1
The court structure

A   CRIMINAL COURTS

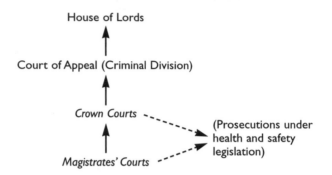

House of Lords

Court of Appeal (Criminal Division)

Crown Courts

(Prosecutions under health and safety legislation)

Magistrates' Courts

B   CIVIL COURTS AND TRIBUNALS

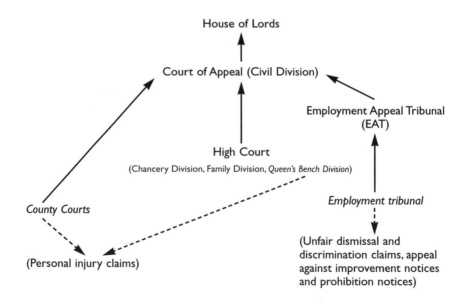

House of Lords

Court of Appeal (Civil Division)

Employment Appeal Tribunal (EAT)

High Court
(Chancery Division, Family Division, *Queen's Bench Division*)

Employment tribunal

County Courts

(Personal injury claims)

(Unfair dismissal and discrimination claims, appeal against improvement notices and prohibition notices)

APPENDIX 2

DSM-IV – Diagnostic criteria for post-traumatic stress disorder

A The person has been exposed to a traumatic event in which both of the following were present:

(1) the person experienced, witnessed or was confronted with an event or events that involved actual or threatened death or serious injury, or a threat to the physical integrity of self or others.

(2) the person's response involved intense fear, helplessness or horror. Note: In children, this may be expressed instead by disorganised or agitated behaviour.

B The traumatic event is persistently re-experienced in one (or more) of the following ways:

(1) recurrent and intrusive distressing recollections of the event, including images, thoughts or perceptions. Note: In young children, repetitive play may occur in which themes or aspects of the trauma are expressed.

(2) recurrent distressing dreams of the event. Note: In children, there may be frightening dreams without recognisable content.

(3) acting or feeling as if the traumatic event were recurring (includes a sense of reliving the experience, illusions, hallucinations and dissociative flashback episodes including those that occur on awakening or when intoxicated). Note: In young children, trauma-specific re-enactment may occur.

(4)   intense psychological distress at exposure to internal or external cues that symbolise or resemble an aspect of the traumatic event.

(5)   physiological reactivity on exposure to internal or external cues that symbolise or resemble an aspect of the traumatic event.

C   Persistent avoidance of stimuli associated with the trauma and numbing of general responsiveness (not present before the trauma), as indicated by three (or more) of the following:

(1)   efforts to avoid thoughts, feelings or conversations associated with trauma

(2)   efforts to avoid activities, places or people that arouse recollections of the trauma

(3)   inability to recall an important aspect of the trauma

(4)   markedly diminished interest or participation in significant activities

(5)   feeling of detachment or estrangement from others

(6)   restricted range of affect (eg unable to have loving feelings)

(7)   sense of foreshortened future (eg does not expect to have a career, marriage, children or a normal life span).

D   Persistent symptoms of increased arousal (not present before the trauma), as indicated by two (or more) of the following:

(1)   difficulty falling or staying asleep

(2)   irritability or outbursts of anger

(3)   difficulty concentrating

(4)   hypervigilance

(5)   exaggerated startle response.

E   Duration of the disturbance (symptoms in Criteria B, C and D) is more than one month.

F   The disturbance causes clinically significant distress or impairment in social, occupational or other important areas of functioning.

Specify if:
Acute: if duration of symptoms is less than three months
Chronic: if duration of symptoms is three months or more.

Source: American Psychiatric Association. *Diagnostic and Statistical Manual of Mental Disorders.* 4th edn. International Version, Washington, D.C., American Psychiatric Association, 1995.

APPENDIX 3

Criminal injuries compensation

THE TARIFF SCHEME (Effective from 1 April 1994)

Relevant sections:

Personal injury
8.3 To qualify for an award of compensation you must have suffered a physical or mental injury, sufficiently serious to be classified in one of the Tariff bands attached to the scheme.

Directly attributable
8.4 You will only be compensated for injuries directly resulting from a crime of violence. This means that we must satisfy ourselves, on the basis of all the facts, that not only was the incident in which you were injured a crime of violence, but also that the incident was the substantial cause of your injury.

Trespass on a railway
8.8 If you were employed by a railway company and were present and saw another person injured or killed as a result of trespassing on the railway you may be entitled to compensation for the shock you suffered. You may also be entitled if you discovered a body on or beside the track or were involved in the immediate aftermath of the incident. [As in 8.3 above, shock must be sufficiently serious.]

Tariff of injuries (Not at present in operation due to successful challenge in the courts, ie there is not a fixed sum for a given injury. However the tariff may be reintroduced in the future.)

SHOCK – disabling mental disorder where the psychological and/or physical symptoms **AND** disability persist for more than six weeks from the incident.

	Band	Tariff payment (£)
Moderate – lasting for 6 to 16 weeks	1	1,000
Serious – lasting for 16 to 26 weeks	9	4,000
Severe – lasting over 26 weeks but not permanent	12	7,500
Very severe – permanent disability (excluding also physical symptoms for which the maximum award is Band 12)	17	20,000

Shock or 'nervous shock' may be taken to include conditions attributed to PTSD, depression and similar generic terms covering such psychological symptoms as anxiety, tension, insomnia, irritability, loss of confidence, agoraphobia, preoccupation with thoughts of self-harm or guilt and related physical ones such as alopecia, asthma, eczema, enuresis and psoriasis. *Disability* in this context will include *impaired work* (or school) *performance*, significant adverse effects on social relationships and sexual dysfunction.

APPENDIX 4

Workplace stress questionnaire

WORKPLACE STRESS CLAIMS

Please answer the following questions.

1   Is your firm involved in any personal injury claim in which workplace stress was the cause of the injury? (Circle appropriate response)

    Yes
    No

2   If the answer to question 1 was YES, please state the number of such claims in which your firm is involved.

    . . . .

3   Please fill in the following chart for each claim, using the key overleaf:

	CLAIM 1	CLAIM 2	CLAIM 3	CLAIM 4	CLAIM 5	CLAIM 6
A						
B						
C						
D						
E						
F						
G						
H						
I						
J						
K						
L						

A = Factor causing stress (eg bullying, long hours)
B = Nature of 'injury' (eg nervous breakdown)
C = Employee still employed by respondent? (Yes/No)
D = Sector? (Private/public)
E = Nature of employee's job
F = Union backing? (Yes/No)
G = Medical report obtained? (Yes/No)
H = Counsel's opinion obtained? (Yes/No)
I = Employee granted legal aid? (Yes/No)
J = Estimated chance of success (%)
K = Decision taken not to pursue? (Yes/No)
L = Claim settled? (Yes/No) If YES, how much?

4   Which of the following factors would tend to deter you from pursuing a stress claim? (TICK ALL APPLICABLE)

 (i) Employee not backed by union
 (ii) Employee has history of mental illness/instability
(iii) Employee suffered stress symptoms but no clinically diagnosable
       condition

(iv) Employee never complained to management
(v)   Other (Please specify)

THANK YOU FOR YOUR TIME. PLEASE RETURN YOUR
QUESTIONNAIRE TO US IN THE ENCLOSED ENVELOPE.

APPENDIX 5

UMIST's policy on the protection of dignity for men and women at work

UMIST strives to be an equal opportunity employer and has operated a formal equal opportunities policy since 1986.

This document is intended to complement the existing equal opportunities policy by setting out UMIST's policy on the protection of the dignity of men and women at work.

The policy is intended to help all members of staff deal with any incident of harassment and to develop a working environment in which harassment is known to be unacceptable and individuals are confident enough to bring complaints without fear of ridicule or reprisal.

Any incidents of harassment will be regarded very seriously and may lead to disciplinary action up to and including dismissal.

What is harassment?

Harassment can be defined as behaviour that is unwanted and that results in the creation of a stressful or intimidating environment for the recipient. This can include unwelcome physical, verbal or non-verbal conduct.

People who are perceived as different, who are in a minority or who lack organisational power run the greatest risk of being harassed.

A range of behaviour may constitute harassment. It is unacceptable if it is unwanted and offensive to the recipient.

UMIST is committed to eradicating all forms of unacceptable behaviour at work. Harassment creates an intimidating, hostile and humiliating work environment for those affected and can have a devastating effect on health, confidence and morale. The anxiety of and stress on the individual can also lead to increased absenteeism, reduced performance and increased staff turnover.

The commonest forms of harassment are outlined below.

1 Sexual harassment

Sexual harassment is a form of unlawful sex discrimination. Sexual harassment occurs in a variety of situations that share a common element: the inappropriate introduction of sexual activities or comments into the work environment. It frequently involves the abuse of an unequal power relationship and contains an element of coercion. Examples of sexual harassment include:

☐ unnecessary and unwelcome physical contact
☐ suggestive and unwelcome comments or gestures emphasising the sexuality of an individual or group
☐ speculation about sexual activities
☐ lewd comments about dress or appearance
☐ unwelcome requests for socio-sexual encounters/favours
☐ displaying sexually offensive material in the workplace
☐ criminal acts such as indecent exposure, sexual harassment, malicious phone calls, etc.

Sexual harassment is unlawful where a person's rejection of, or submission to, such behaviour may be used as the basis for decisions that affect that person's employment (including access to training, promotion, salary increases or any other employment decision), or where such behaviour creates an intimidating, hostile or offensive working environment.

Sexual attention becomes harassment if it is persisted in when either it has been made clear by the recipient that it is unwanted or offensive or when such would be evident to a reasonable person.

Some specific groups have proved particularly susceptible to sexual harassment, often due to their perceived vulnerability in the eyes of their harassers. Those disproportionately at risk include: divorced or separated women; young men and new entrants to the labour market; those with short-term or temporary contracts; women in non-traditional jobs; women with disabilities; lesbians; and women from ethnic minorities. Among men, gay men and young men are particularly vulnerable to harassment.

2 Racial harassment

Racial harassment is a form of unlawful racial discrimination. It is an act or series of acts directed towards an individual because of his or her race, colour or ethnic origin. Such behaviour includes:

□ derogatory name-calling, verbal abuse and threats
□ insults and racist jokes
□ ridicule of an individual for cultural differences
□ exclusion from normal workplace conversations or social events
□ unfair allocation of work and responsibilities
□ racist graffiti or insignia
□ physical assault.

Differences of attitude or culture and the misinterpretation of social signals can mean that what is perceived as racial harassment by one person may not seem so to another. The defining features of racial harassment, however, are that the behaviour is offensive or intimidating to the recipient and would be regarded as racial harassment by any reasonable person. Racial harassment is unlawful when any such behaviour creates an intimidating, hostile or offensive working environment.

3 Other forms of harassment

There are other forms of harassment that can equally cause misery for the recipient. Such harassment may include:

□ behaviour that makes direct or indirect reference to disability or impairment
□ bullying and insults
□ unfounded criticism of the performance of work tasks
□ persistent teasing, pranks and practical jokes because of personal characteristics or traits, including age, religion, etc
□ persistent pressure to become involved in anti-social or criminal behaviour.

Stopping harassment is your responsibility

Managers, colleagues, friends, union representatives and the personnel office all have a responsibility for ensuring that individuals do not suffer any form of harassment and that they are encouraged and supported if they wish to make a legitimate complaint.

Witnesses of such incidents should offer support as necessary to the person experiencing the harassment. There may also be circumstances in which a witness brings forward a complaint against the harasser.

Managers have a particular responsibility to ensure that harassment does not occur in the area of work for which they are responsible. Managers should also be responsive and supportive to any member of staff who complains about harassment, provide full and clear advice on the procedure to be adopted, maintain confidentiality and ensure that there is no further problem of harassment or victimisation after the complaint has been resolved.

How to deal with harassment

It is a distinguishing characteristic of harassment that recipients are often reluctant to complain. Sometimes they think that there is no point complaining, because nothing will be done, or because it will be trivialised, or that they will suffer ridicule or reprisal.

If you feel you are being subjected to harassment in any form, do not feel that it is your fault or that you have to tolerate it.

Harassment is recognised as a serious issue and will be treated as such by UMIST. Harassment in any form will not be permitted or condoned.

There are various ways in which you can deal with harassment. In many cases, it will be sufficient to ask the harasser to stop. Alternatively, you can seek guidance or make a complaint in confidence, either formally or informally, using the procedures outlined below. Confidential help and advice can be obtained at any stage from the staff welfare officer, the personnel office or from your trade union.

Informal procedures

In many cases, it will be sufficient for the person being harassed to ask the harasser to stop, particularly where the harassment was unintentional. A swift and clear indication that the behaviour is objectionable will often prove effective.

The request to stop should be made face-to-face wherever possible. However, the request could alternatively be made in writing or through a third party (eg line manager, colleague, staff welfare officer, personnel office or trade union official).

If this informal route fails to resolve the problem, the person being harassed may wish to keep a record of the incidents involved, the dates on which harassment occurred and any attempts to confront the harasser, in preparation for making a formal complaint.

Counselling

Sometimes, for whatever reason, an individual will decide not to make a formal complaint about harassment, but will still need help in resolving the situation and coping with the stress that harassment causes.

UMIST also provides a staff counselling service free to all employees. The professional external counsellor can help to provide advice and support to those who have suffered harassment. Appointments can be made via the occupational health service.

Formal procedures

Where a formal complaint is made, all allegations will be investigated swiftly, fairly and confidentially under UMIST's grievance procedure. Employees bringing forward complaints of harassment will be protected against consequent victimisation and retaliation.

In certain circumstances it might be appropriate to bypass the early stages of the formal grievance procedure. This would apply where the individual is unable to discuss the complaint with their immediate manager (eg where the manager is the alleged harasser). There may also be circumstances where particular sensitivities make the individual reluctant to take the matter to the head of department. At any time, the individual may pursue the alternative route of discussing the problem with a member of the personnel office.

Where harassment is found to have taken place, disciplinary action will be taken as appropriate. Perpetrators of harassment may be dismissed where misconduct is serious. Certain types of harassment are also criminal offences (eg assault). Instances of subsequent intimidation and victimisation will also be disciplinary offences.

Where a complaint is upheld, redeployment may be a desirable outcome, although it will not always be practicable. Where redeployment is considered, the complainant will be given the choice, wherever possible, to remain in post or to transfer. Even where a complaint is not upheld, for example because evidence is not regarded as conclusive, redeployment may still provide an alternative to requiring the parties to continue to work together against their wishes.

UMIST also recognises that there is a possibility that complaints might be brought with mischievous or malicious intent. Such misconduct may provide grounds for disciplinary action up to and including dismissal.

Criminal offences

Many forms of harassment may amount to criminal behaviour since any kind of unwanted physical contact, or the apprehension of it, could constitute an assault or indecent assault.

Staff are strongly urged to consider reporting such behaviour to the police without delay, so that a criminal investigation can be carried out and the due judicial processes followed.

UMIST may also take separate action in cases of gross misconduct, although it reserves the right to suspend internal disciplinary action pending the outcome of any criminal charges.

APPENDIX 6
Useful addresses

HSE Books
PO Box 1999
Sudbury
Suffolk CO10 2WA
Tel: 01787 881165

Mind (The National Association for Mental Health)
Granta House
15-19 Broadway
Stratford
London E15 4BQ
Tel: 08457 660 163

Defeat Depression in the Workplace
Royal College of Psychiatrists
17 Belgrave Square
London SW1X 8PG
(booklets available)
Tel: 020 7235 2351

SANE
2nd Floor
199-205 Old Marylebone Road
London NW1 5PQ
Tel: 020 7742 6520

Equal Opportunities Commission
Arndale House
Arndale Centre
Manchester M4 3EQ
(for eg queries on harassment policies)
Tel: 0161 833 9244

European Foundation for the Improvement of Living and Working
Conditions
Loughlinstown House
Shankhill
Co. Dublin
Ireland
(EC body concerned with workplace issues such as stress)

APPENDIX 7

Trade union policy on PTSD

1 MSF

a Employees should be involved in development of prevention of violence at work strategy.

b Risk assessment to uncover hazards is required.

c Employers' action plan should isolate problems, report all incidents, classify those incidents, develop preventative measures and enact those measures while evaluating the success/changes required.

d Safety representatives have a role in conducting workplace surveys and overseeing the operation of training schemes.

e Safety representatives have a further checking role in ensuring the policy is disseminated and ensuring that shortcomings are reported back to management.

f MSF believe staffing levels have been reduced with inappropriate consideration to health and safety risks. Furthermore, job design has exacerbated those risks.

g MSF recommends personal security measures and extensive advice to staff on travelling to and from work/home visits which puts them at risk.

h MSF insists employers develop comprehensive after-care procedures for staff experiencing violence at work, including full investigations; counselling; further specialist help where required; procedural review; information provided to the victim; time off work with full pay; and assistance in claiming compensation. The union holds model policies for these issues.

2 BIFU

a BIFU has worked closely with the Health and Safety Executive in the development of new guidelines for preventing armed robberies in financial services.

b BIFU therefore presses employers to adopt the guidelines and singles out some specific areas for action.

c The union has asked the Home Office to warn the public not to carry imitation firearms and is pressing for recognition of such behaviour to constitute a serious offence where there is no good reason for so doing.

d It seeks to raise the profile of such issues in a more sensitive manner than is currently the case owing to media coverage.

e BIFU has undertaken to work with financial service institutions to secure a better working environment.

f Specific concerns include education and training; after-care counselling; co-ordinated security policy; physical protection; surveillance equipment; and liaison with the police.

(*Violence at Work*, IDS Study, July 1994: 11/12, 14/15.)

APPENDIX 8

Further reading

COOPER C. L. (ed.). *Handbook of Stress, Medicine and Health*. Boca Ratan, Florida, CRC Press, 1996.

COOPER C. L. and PALMER S. *Conquer Your Stress*. London, IPD, 1999.

COOPER C. L. and STRAW A. *Successful Stress Management*. London, Hodder Headline, 1994.

'Health promotion in the workplace: parts 1 and 2'. *IRS Employment Trends*. 554/555, February/March 1994.

NAPIER M. and WHEAT K. *Recovering Damages for Psychiatric Injury*. London, Blackstone, 1995.

'Stress, health and work'. *Health and Safety Information Bulletin*. 220, April 1994.

SUTHERLAND V. *and* COOPER C. L. Strategic Stress Management. London, Macmillan Books, 1999.

'Violence against employees – a legal perspective'. *Health and Safety Information Bulletin*. 218, February 1994.

LIST OF CASES

ACTR   Australian Capital Territory Reports
All ER   All England Law Reports
ICR   Industrial Case Reports
IRLIB   Industrial Relations Legal Information Bulletin
IRLR   Industrial Relations Law Reports
LR   Law Reports
NLJ   New Law Journal
PIQR   Personal Injuries and Quantum Reports

LIST OF STATUTES AND REGULATIONS

British legislation

Administration of Justice Act 1982
Congenital Disabilities Act 1976
Control of Substances Hazardous to Health Regulations 1988
Disability Discrimination Act (DDA) 1995
Disability Discrimination (Employment) Regulations 1996
Disability Discrimination (Meaning of Disability) Regulations 1996
Employers' Liability (Compulsory Insurance) Act 1969
Employment Relations Act 1999
Employment Rights Act (ERA) 1996
Fair Employment (Northern Ireland) Act 1976
Health and Safety at Work Act (HASAWA) 1974
Health and Safety (Display Screen Equipment) Regulations 1992
Industrial Tribunals Act 1996
Latent Damage Act 1986
Limitation Act 1980
Management of Health and Safety at Work Regulations (MHSW) 1992
Mental Health Act 1983
Offences Against the Person Act 1861
Offences Against the Person Act 1986
Protection from Harassment Act 1997
Race Relations Act (RRA) 1976
Race Relations (Remedies) Act 1994
Sex Discrimination Act (SDA) 1975
Sex Discrimination and Equal Pay (Remedies) Regulations 1993
Supreme Court Act 1981
Unfair Contract Terms Act 1977
Working Time Regulations 1998

European legislation

EU Working Time Directive 93/104/23

INDEX